995

The Graduate School Funding Handbook

The Graduate School Funding Handbook

April Vahle Hamel

with Mary Morris Heiberger
and Julia Miller Vick

University of Pennsylvania Press

Philadelphia

Library of Congress Cataloging-in-Publication Data
Hamel, April Vahle.
   The graduate school funding handbook / April Vahle Hamel with Mary
Morris Heiberger and Julia Miller Vick.
      p.   cm.
   Includes bibliographical references and index.
   ISBN 0–8122–3232–1. — ISBN 0–8122–1447–1 (pbk.)
   1. Universities and colleges—United States—Graduate work—
Finance.   2. Graduate students—Scholarships, fellowships, etc.—
United States.   I. Heiberger, Mary Morris.   II. Vick, Julia
Miller.   III. Title.
LB2371.4.H35   1994
378.3—dc20   94-28902
                                                                    CIP

378.3
1212

Contents

154, 157

7. Postdoctoral Fellowships   137

Mary Morris Heiberger and Julia Miller Vick

Chapter 1
Graduate Degrees, Institutional Financial Aid, and Application Tips

The purpose of this book is to cast light on the murky world of graduate school funding. Our conversations with undergraduates and other potential graduate school applicants make it clear that institutions offer piecemeal information, at best, about institutional as well as external funding. Acquiring reliable information about types of degrees and what they mean is also difficult.

In this chapter, we will look at the bare essentials of graduate education: graduate degree types, the nature of institutional financial aid and external financial aid, the affordability of graduate school, and tips on applying to graduate programs. Subsequent chapters will examine external funding opportunities and grant/fellowship proposal writing strategies in more detail.

Types of Graduate Degrees

In 1994, over 1.5 million students were enrolled in graduate programs around the United States. In any given year, graduate schools can expect to award a total of approximately 350,000 master's degrees, 75,000 first professional degrees, and 40,000 doctoral degrees, a total number of nearly 500,000 graduate degrees per year. Not all these programs function in the same way, nor do they provide the same amounts and types of funding.

Given the enormous number of students enrolled in graduate degree programs, it is important that we refine the categories of degree possibilities if we are going to understand them. We have classified graduate programs into the general categories described in the rest of this section. Table 1 at the end of the section provides a summary of this information. To understand the rest of the book, you will need to understand the characteristics of the programs in which you have an interest.

Master's Programs

Applied/professional master's programs require one to three years of coursework and are constructed to prepare people for careers in the professions. Such programs as master's degrees in business administration (MBA), teaching (MAT), and social work (MSW), and others fall into this category. Many of these courses of study include some sort of internship or hands-on experience. For example, schools of social work usually require a practicum as part of the curriculum. Experience in the profession between undergraduate school and graduate school matriculation is also often highly desirable. Business schools generally prefer applicants who have had some business-related work experience.

Research master's programs require one to two years of coursework and are designed to enhance the research experience begun in undergraduate school by bringing previously learned investigative skills to a more sophisticated level. For completion of the degree requirement, some programs require that the student construct a long research paper called a *thesis*; in addition, most expect successful performance in written or oral examinations and possibly a series of papers and examinations. Most research master's programs (MA, MS) in the arts and sciences (English, history, political science, biology, etc.) fall into this category. Students in these programs usually wish to extend their knowledge in a field in order to prepare for doctoral work or to improve their job prospects in a particular area; occasionally, they enroll for the sake of knowledge. Students who enter these programs can expect to do a significant amount of research and paper writing.

Creative master's programs last two to three years and are intended to expand on the creative education started in undergraduate school or through other experience. Painters, photographers, musicians, poets, and artists of all sorts are attracted to creative programs in the fine arts (MFA), music (MM), writing and poetry (MFAW) and others. Creative programs usually require a project such as a book of poetry, a recital, or an exhibition as a graduation requirement. While students in these fields may have multiple career aims, all usually intend to continue their creative work in addition, perhaps, to teaching at a variety of levels or working in a related field. Graduates with these degrees often acquire teaching certification for elementary or secondary education careers or pursue a research doctorate in the same or a related field; an MFAW (writing) graduate, for example, may eventually seek a PhD in

English with the intention of writing fiction while teaching at the college level.

Doctoral Programs

Applied/professional doctoral programs such as those found in business (DBA), medicine (MD), law (JD), and education (EdD), like their master's counterparts, are designed to develop a corps of new professionals who will apply their skills in a hands-on style. Graduates with these degrees may stay on to teach or do research in a college or university, but most aim at a career outside higher education. An MD, for example, may practice medicine in a private, group, or institutional practice, do full-time clinical teaching or research at a medical school, or combine clinical practice and teaching, but most MDs will spend most of their careers in clinical practice.

The length of study in these programs ranges from three to four years (although degrees in education often take longer because they are usually carried out on a part-time basis). The requirements for completion may include a practicum, such as the clinical years in medicine or summer internships in law, or may entail the development of a complex project that is written up and submitted for scrutiny. The applied doctorate may additionally require postdoctoral experience or passing national licensing examinations as a prerequisite for active participation in the profession. Medicine requires at least a year of postgraduate internship and, depending upon the field, further training in residencies. Both law and medicine have postgraduate examinations—on a national level for medicine and on a state level for law.

The **research doctorate** almost always culminates in the awarding of a PhD. (Although the degree stands for "doctor of philosophy," it is awarded in almost all research doctoral fields. It is always followed by a qualification, such as "Doctor of Philosophy in French.") While most research doctoral degree programs are found in the arts and sciences or engineering, they are also available in business, social work, and other professional areas. Students in these programs usually intend to do research in higher education (colleges and universities), industry, or government, or they plan to teach at the college or university level. In many instances a combination of research and teaching is the predictable career result.

The length of time needed to complete a research doctorate ranges from four to eight years depending on the discipline. Students spend two to three years in coursework, one to three years doing research in a field within the discipline (for example, nineteenth-century intellectual history within history) and then one to three years writing a major research paper called a *dissertation*. A dissertation may range in length from 100 to 700 pages.

Students in the sciences usually finish much more quickly than those in the humanities because scientists ordinarily select their field very quickly and engage in dissertation research within the first two to three years of their programs. Humanities students spend time taking a range of courses and may not turn to field research until the third or fourth year; even then they may not pick a topic for another year or more. Certainly there are students in the humanities who are very focused on entry into their programs and who finish within five years, but, on average, graduate study in the humanities takes longer.

It is hard to generalize about the time it takes to get a degree in the social sciences because of the varied natures of the disciplines within this division. While an economics degree might take five or six years to complete, a program in anthropology could take longer because of the extensive fieldwork required. In general, the PhD completion speed is determined by the focus and organization of the program as well as the individual student. The same program at the same school might find student *A* finishing in five years and student *B* nine years.

Applicants are sometimes confused about whether they have to get a master's degree before applying to a doctoral program. In most cases the answer is no. One can apply directly to a PhD or other type of doctoral program with nothing more than a bachelor's degree (in hand or about to be received). In some doctoral programs, people who intend to complete the doctoral degree will first be enrolled as master's students and, when they successfully complete their examinations, will automatically be recategorized as doctoral students. Sometimes a person will get a master's degree, work for awhile, and then embark on a course of doctoral study. In most cases, some credit will be given toward the doctorate based on the master's if the field and the programs are compatible. When an institution's guidelines give the *time to degree* in a doctoral program as four to eight years, that represents the total time it takes the average student to go from being a first-year graduate student to completing the doctoral degree requirements. In many doctoral programs, a master's degree is awarded, almost automatically, after the completion of 30 or more credit hours.

At specified points in each program, doctoral students take a series of written and oral examinations. Sometimes these tests are called *qualifying examinations* and must be passed within the first two years of the program as a prerequisite for continuing to a doctoral degree. This system is common, for example, in economics. In other programs *comprehensive examinations* are taken after the completion of coursework. Success in the examinations is required before the student may construct a dissertation proposal.

Although the time to degree is shorter on average in the sciences, it is usual for those graduates to enter a postdoctoral training program. *Postdoctorates* are those years after doctoral degree graduation when a person is still engaged in learning new techniques, doing research under the guidance of a mentor, or perhaps independently enhancing academic credentials through publication. They are transitional training years that bridge the gap from graduate work to full entry-level standing within the profession. The length of these "postdocs," as they are called, varies from one to five years depending on the discipline. While postdocs are not as common in the social sciences and humanities, they are becoming more prevalent in these fields as time goes on.

Combined Degree Programs

Combining applied and research degree programs is not unusual. A master's student in social work may simultaneously pursue a law degree; a medical student may be engaged in a concurrent PhD program in biology. The medical student may spend the first two years in medical school, then do two years of research in biology, and then return to medical school to do two years of clinical medicine. Combined programs are not always emphasized in an institution's programmatic literature and, in many instances, may be specially arranged to suit a particular student's interest. If you are interested in a combined degree you should be sure to ask whether such a program is possible. Ordinarily, applications are submitted to both programs, and the applicant must be accepted by both. Occasionally, an established combined program may require only a single application.

Certificate Programs

It is not uncommon for universities to offer certificates or programs that will satisfy state or other agency certification requirements. In some cases, the certificate may be related to licensing requirements within the field. People in education may need a number of certifications in order to work as teachers, counselors, or administrators, and universities can provide the courses that satisfy these requirements.

Other certificates may not lead to licensing or to a degree but may simply be a university's way of giving recognition to the acquisition of skills or information in a particular area. For example, certification in women's studies may mean that a doctoral student in French literature

TABLE 1. Types of Degree Programs and Sampling of Degrees Offered

Types of programs	Sampling of degrees offered	
Master's		
Applied/professional	**MABM**	Master of Agribusiness Management
	MAdmJ	Master in Administration of Justice
	MAMB	Master of Applied Molecular Biology
	MAP	Master of Applied Psychology
	MAPA	Master of Arts in Public Administration
	MArch	Master of Architecture
	MBA	Master of Business Administration
	MSW	Master of Social Work
Research	**MA**	Master of Arts (most common, e.g., anthropology, English, history, international studies, public policy)
	MS	Master of Science (e.g., chemistry, mathematics, physics)
Creative	**MFA**	Master of Fine Arts (e.g., furniture design, photography, painting, sculpture)
	MFAW	Master of Fine Arts in Writing
	MM	Master of Music (e.g., composing, performance)
Doctoral		
Applied/professional	**DBA**	Doctor of Business Administration
	DC	Doctor of Chiropractic
	DEd **(EdD)**	Doctor of Education
	DDS	Doctor of Dental Surgery
	DScA	Doctor of Applied Science
	DVM	Doctor of Veterinary Medicine
	MD	Doctor of Medicine
Research	**DSc**	Doctor of Science
	DTh	Doctor of Theology
	PhD	Doctor of Philosophy (most common, e.g., art history, economics, English literature, molecular biology, physics, psychology, social work)

has satisfied the university's requirements within an area of concentration. The certificate is viewed as an enhancement to the degree program.

Institutional Financial Aid

General Information

Financial aid available to graduate students from or through universities comes in many forms. The types of funding accessible and how aid is distributed can vary drastically from what is available through the undergraduate system. In general, however, like undergraduate funding, monies for graduate scholarships and fellowships that are offered by institutions to students are allocated on the basis of *need, merit,* or a *need/merit combination.*

Professional schools tend to make need the primary barometer for determining which applicants are given financial support. Financial need means that applicants do not own property over a certain value or have income over a stipulated amount—in other words, that they are living in a state of relative poverty. While certainly rank in the applicant pool can influence the size of the scholarship, or even whether a scholarship will be granted, students who are given institutional funds must almost always pass a financial needs test. Simply put, if an applicant personally owns a condo in Florida, has a stock portfolio, and drives a BMW, scholarship offers to business school are not likely even for those who rank high in the applicant pool. Most applied master's and doctoral programs also follow this example.

There are, of course, some exceptions to this rule. One notable exception occurs when administrators are trying to improve the institution's ranked position—that is, when they are trying to raise the institution program to a higher position of regard relative to its peer programs. It is not unusual for a school or program to offer a large chunk of money to the very best prospects who apply, regardless of need. Through this financial inducement, they hope, applicants who might normally enroll in a top five or top ten institution enroll in the lower-ranked program. Applicants should look for these opportunities and balance the type of education that is possible and the career placement prospects with the financial incentives.

Arts and sciences master's and doctoral programs generally award scholarships and fellowships based primarily on merit. That is, applicants are ranked against one another for admissions based on their past scholarly performance or on their future academic potential. Financial need is not a factor. In some instances, however, a student who has been made a merit offer of funds must also pass a needs test. These circumstances can be driven by outside pressures. The U.S. Department of Education, for example, gives blocks of training grant money to selected departments at numerous universities. When the departments underwrite incoming or continuing students with these resources, they must make sure that the recipients have passed a standardized needs test.

It is not unusual for a university's departments or schools to have more than one set of funding criteria. Business schools usually fund MBA students on a need-based system, for example, while PhD students are funded on a merit-based or combined arrangement.

Two separate issues in graduate education drive student funding considerations: first, how the program is financed and, second, how many years students are expected to remain in the program and what career path they usually follow.

In most professional schools, incoming student tuition keeps the enterprise going; faculty salaries and the expenses incurred to run student service programs such as career centers are paid for out of these resources. Consequently, the school must take in a certain amount of tuition money in order to offer graduate degrees; this is the same principal that drives undergraduate admissions. Under this assumption, professional schools make financial offers to the extent they feel applicants can afford to pay a percentage of the tuition. A financial assistance offer from the average professional school is designed to make the program affordable enough that the prospective student will enroll and pay some level of tuition. The aim is a sort of balanced reciprocity based on the needs of the student and the institution.

In addition, students who enter most professions after graduate work (social work, fine arts, and others aside) are expected to earn fairly substantial incomes. That is certainly the promise of careers in business, law, and medicine. This group are usually in school for two to four years, a relatively shorter period of time than most research doctoral students, and also often have the opportunity to earn substantial income in the summer. These students, so the conventional wisdom goes, can afford to pay their way through graduate school based on their potential earnings. Loans, therefore, become the primary source of financial aid for these scholars. (Not all institutions adhere to this notion, however. In recent years a few medical schools have committed themselves to providing "no tuition" training.)

Student financial allocations are viewed differently in research doctoral programs, especially in the arts and sciences. First, undergraduate tuition is used to fund graduate as well as undergraduate programs. This is especially true when graduate students are given stipends to act as teaching assistants in undergraduate classes. There certainly are universities where graduate tuition is an important component of financing programs and where students are expected to pay for their education, but this condition tends to be found in non-doctoral degree granting institutions where the master's programs are more applied than research-oriented. Other exceptions include the most competitive and prestigious doctoral-granting institutions, which may admit people who aim to be doctoral students on a trial basis as master's students and charge them the regular tuition, at least for the first year.

All these exceptions aside, most research doctoral students are not expected to support themselves through their entire tenure in graduate school because they are in their programs much too long, they perform important services in educating undergraduates and in helping to facilitate faculty research, and they have limited postgraduation earning potential. A doctoral graduate in English can expect to take six to eight years to complete his or her degree and then go on to a full-time, tenure track position that pays between $28,000 and $35,000 a year with the prospect of only cost of living increases for the next seven years. This graduate cannot afford to pay back $75,000 in loans. To reasonably expect to recruit students into long-term programs with such limited earning potential, universities must offer at least some form of solid financial, no-payback support to the most qualified students.

Private and public universities often approach doctoral student funding differently, offering different combinations of fellowships, assistantships, and loans. State institutions may not be able to provide funding to students for as many years as private institutions. Nevertheless, doctoral students at all types of universities should anticipate receiving substantial merit-based support. Any doctoral applicant who is not offered good support should seriously consider looking at other institutions or other career paths.

Tuition Scholarships

Tuition scholarships (sometimes called tuition remission or tuition waivers) are meant to reduce the amount of tuition a student has to pay. In some cases a tuition scholarship will cover the entire tuition bill; in others it will take care of only part of the costs. No money changes hands, and the award is not considered taxable income, and students are not expected to pay it back. Students may get a non-negotiable tuition voucher, which they then present at registration. When applying to all types of master's and doctoral programs, you should inquire about the availability of tuition scholarships and whether they are awarded on a need or merit basis. In some areas, such as arts and sciences, these scholarships are very common, especially for doctoral students.

Fellowships

Fellowships are actual dollars paid beyond tuition scholarships. These monies are meant to support students by making money available to cover room, board, books, and supplies and are taxable as income. Full fellowship amounts for the 1995–1996 academic year are expected to be within a mid-range of $7,500 to $10,500 for nine months of support (some programs support students on a twelve-month basis and the stipend will be proportionately higher). The rate can be expected to go up, on average, by $500 per year.

The money is generally referred to as a *stipend*. There is no payback expected, and a student is not required to work for these funds (although some training grant fellowships have a payback component if the student does not stay in the field for a certain length of time after graduation). Fellowships are usually offered by universities for the first year of study and, less often, for the last year of dissertation writing. They are given to master's and doctoral students in all types of programs but are found most often in doctoral programs in research fields. Fellowships almost always come from the university the student is attending, but sometimes a student may apply to an outside agency such as the National Science Foundation or the Department of Education for *portable fellowships*, which may be taken to any graduate institution.

Assistantships

An assistantship is a form of funding that requires some performance of duties in exchange for a stipend. The stipend is usually much larger than would ordinarily be paid for the type of work done. Students who function as teaching assistants, for example, are commonly expected to help with an undergraduate course for, on average, twelve hours a week; for this service, they are paid up to $5,000 a semester. A part-time instructor teaching a single course with full responsibility would not normally be paid anywhere near that amount of money.

There are three forms of assistantships: teaching, research, and graduate assistantships. They are found in the greatest numbers in engineering and arts and sciences programs, but professional programs also offer assistantships. Depending on the type of institution and the programs it offers, both master's and doctoral students may be eligible for these stipends.

Teaching Assistantships

A teaching assistantship requires that a student spend from five to twenty hours a week assisting a professor with classes or independently teaching a course. The former is more common than the latter. Teaching assistants (TAs) supervise laboratories, run discussion sections, assign and grade written assignments, proctor and grade examinations, drill language students, help with equipment, tutor undergraduates, hold office hours, and lecture in class. With the exception of laboratory supervision and language drilling, most TAs perform all these functions to one degree or another at one time or another. In most large state and some private universities, TAs are responsible for handling a great deal of the instructional load. This is especially true in large institutions and those with serious financial constraints. The use of great numbers of teaching assistants has come in for intense criticism in recent times, and teaching assistants have, in the past, often felt exploited. Fortunately, universities have begun in the last decade to develop more comprehensive TA training programs.

The money to support TA stipends comes, primarily, from tuition paid by undergraduate or graduate students at private universities and from state appropriations at public universities. Teaching assistantship stipends are expected to be within a mid-range of $8,500–$10,500 a year for nine months, plus waiver of tuition and fees, during the 1995–1996 academic year. The rate usually goes up approximately $500 per year.

Depending on the university, a student may be required to function as a TA in the first year of matriculation. This is especially true in state institutions. In private universities, a student may receive a work-free fellowship the first year and then act as a TA the second and third years, perhaps longer. While teaching assistantships are available in all types of departments, they are more prevalent in the humanities and social sciences.

Applicants are always curious about how much time is devoted to being a TA and how that time might affect their success in coursework. The answer is not simple and depends on how a particular department within a particular school utilizes TA services. In some areas, the TA experience is viewed as something a student should do for a limited amount of time, perhaps only a year, and for a limited number of hours, probably five to seven hours a week. In departments with lots of training or research grant money, such as the biomedical sciences, being a teaching assistant may be viewed as less important than being a research assistant. In some departments, moreover, teaching acumen is not perceived as crucial to the students' future careers.

In the social sciences and especially in the humanities, the hours a student devotes to being a TA are generally much higher, sometimes 20 or more hours a week. In these departments, undergraduate tuition and undergraduate needs drive the number of hours spent in teaching. English students as well as those in other language and literature disciplines are the people most likely to spend the greatest number of hours functioning as TAs. TAs in composition courses often complain about the amount of time spent in teaching. Many students feel that their time to degree completion is lengthened because of unreasonable teaching expectations.

In some state and private institutions, TAs are considered employees first and students second and may be unionized. In other universities, teaching experience is considered an important part of the curriculum, and teaching assistantships are accordingly conceptualized as academic rather than employment activities. The perspective an institution takes has a great deal to do with how many hours TAs work and what benefits (such as health insurance) they are entitled to. When an assistantship is viewed as a means of providing teaching experience, the hours worked (not more than 18) may be less but the benefits will also probably be less.

When students see themselves as overworked, underpaid, lacking benefits, and being regarded as teaching lackeys, they may unionize, strike, or demonstrate for improved working conditions, better training, and more respect. It is always important that you know how teaching assistantships are viewed by the institutions and departments to which you are applying. Every prospective student should check to see whether there is serious TA unrest before applying to any graduate program. These issues can become very distracting and can poison an atmosphere that should encourage collegiality. You may still decide to attend a university that is experiencing this sort of friction, but you should not do it unwittingly.

The recent literature suggests that being a TA does not necessarily slow down the time it takes to acquire a degree. Many observers believe that being a TA is a beneficial intellectual experience that adds an important socialization component to graduate student life. Students who function as TAs often feel more integrated into their departments as well as into the rest of the academic life of the institution than do those students who do not have teaching assistant opportunities. Most TAs really function as junior faculty and should be respected as such by undergraduates and faculty alike.

Research Assistantships

Research assistantships are found primarily in departments where faculty members have large research grants that include support for students, postdocs, and research associates. Research assistants (RAs) may also be found in areas where large training grants from the federal government are available. These areas are usually in the sciences and engineering, and the sources for research and training grant funding can include the National Institutes of Health, the National Science Foundation, the Department of Defense, and other government agencies, plus corporations such as McDonnell Douglas or Merck that have established important links to academic research. RAs are engaged primarily, but not exclusively, in laboratory research. Generally, this research is seen as part of the curriculum. Consequently, students in the sciences and engineering usually select a field within their discipline fairly quickly so that they can be placed in the appropriate lab. In some programs, students serve in a series of rotations and eventually select their area of specialization. The RA rate is expected to be within a mid-range of \$12,000–\$14,000 for twelve months, plus waiver of tuition and fees, during the 1995–1996 academic year. Rates can be expected to go up, on average, around \$500 per year.

Graduate Assistantships

Another form of assistantship is defined by the catchall term "graduate assistantship." Institutions use graduate assistants (GAs) for all sorts of tasks that do not fit into the TA or RA category. GAs may spend time advising other students on topics ranging from finding part-time jobs to problems encountered by TAs. GAs may edit graduate school newspapers or calculate statistics for admissions. In the best of all worlds, a GA works in an area that enhances his or her academic activities; an education student, for example, might advise teaching assistants or a psychology student might assist in the student counseling center. GA rates are determined at each university and depend upon the nature and duration of the work involved.

College Work-Study

The federal government's College Work-Study Program has funding available through the Graduate and Professional Divisions. Although some of the monies from these programs go to support RAs and TAs, a percentage is usually available to employ students in offices on campus. This employment is not necessarily related to a student's academic interest or to the curriculum. The university is required to contribute to the student's pay; thus the government and the university share the cost of employing students while they are enrolled in coursework. Most universities have federal work-study funds available for students at the graduate as well as undergraduate level.

A graduate program may offer work-study opportunities to individual students or it may make monies accessible to departments that then find students to fill positions. For example, work-study students may work in a graduate school office doing reception work or in an office of international studies doing clerical work. Pay depends on the department, but it is not uncommon for graduate work-study students to earn $7 or $8 per hour or more. Applicants who are not offered fellowships or teaching or research assistantships should always inquire about work-study opportunities. All students must establish financial need through a standardized form available in the graduate school, department, or financial aid office and must be U.S. citizens or permanent residents.

Loans

Loans are more readily available to U.S. citizens or permanent residents than to others. Money is borrowed under the federal government's Stafford Guaranteed Student Loan and the Perkins Direct Student Loan programs. Another congressionally mandated program called the Parent Loans for Undergraduate Students (PLUS) was extended in 1981 to include graduate students.

Getting a loan, like getting college work-study, requires completing forms. These are found in a graduate school or financial aid office on all campuses. While loans must usually be paid back, some programs have a loan forgiveness program. This means that work in a not-for-profit field for a certain number of years after graduation may qualify the graduates for absorption of part or all of the loans. For example, if a law graduate works as a public defender or in a legal aid office for a specified number of years, the university may remove all or part of the loan indebtedness established during law school.

Certainly students should consider their postgraduate earning potential in deciding how much loan indebtedness they can incur.

Summary of Institutional Financial Aid Information

Programs within the same university will have different sorts of financial support packages for their applicants. These may include tuition scholarships, fellowships, assistantships, work-study, and loans. It is important to know what kind of support is available, how long the support can be expected to last, how easy it is to win an award, and the amount of the funding. *No prospective graduate student should go blindly into a program without knowing the short- and long-term financial consequences.*

External Grants and Fellowships

External funding comes from outside the university and is awarded directly to the applicant or student by a private foundation or an agency of the federal government. Sometimes, for accounting purposes, the actual money is filtered through the institution; in other instances the payments are made directly to the students. Applicants should determine whether there is external money available in their area of study. The National Science Foundation, for example, offers 1,000 three-year fellowships for study in engineering, the sciences, or the social sciences. This fellowship pays the student a yearly stipend ($14,000 in 1994) along with all or part of the tuition fees, and can be used at any accredited university.

External funding also exists to encourage underrepresented groups to enroll in graduate programs, especially in the sciences and engineering. Women and members of minority groups should be alert to the variety of these external opportunities.

In some cases money is available through applicants' parents' employers in the form of benefits. Some universities, for example, have tuition benefit plans for the children of faculty and staff, although these usually support only undergraduate education. Certain ethnic organizations offer funding for graduate education. In addition, not-for-profit organizations, such as the Epilepsy Foundation, will support graduate student research.

Much of the rest of this book will examine external opportunities available to applicants and students. Resources that detail external funding opportunities are listed in the Further Reading section at the ends of most chapters.

Companies That Guarantee to Find Funding for Students

Applicants should be wary of mail solicitations from companies that guarantee to find funding for every student. These organizations insist that there is a mother lode of money just waiting to be tapped. In general, most people do not qualify for these sources, which may have oblique requirements such as direct descent from a soldier who fought in the Civil War. The companies usually have a money-back guarantee if the customer does not get a certain amount of money from the foundations described on a list that they provide. But their deal usually requires you to apply to and be rejected by every funding agency on the list before you can get your money back. That could amount to

weeks and sometimes months of work getting applications and applying to, sometimes, over a hundred funding sources with little chance of
receiving an award.

Deciding Whether to Go to Graduate School

Is graduate school right for you? Is it affordable? These are key questions that all prospective graduate students should ask. There are no
simple answers, but there are ways that each individual can determine
whether it makes sense to go to graduate school from an intellectual as
well as a financial perspective. In a way, there is no separating the
intellectual from the financial, but certainly motivation to learn, ambi-
tion to be in a certain career track, and enthusiasm to continue within a
classroom environment are the first topics with which an individual
should deal.

If you are thinking of going to graduate school, you need to do a
thorough self-evaluation. Ask yourself the following questions:

1. Why, specifically, do I want to further my formal education?

2. What do I hope, concretely, to accomplish by acquiring an advanced degree?

3. Am I focused enough on my career track to start graduate school?

4. If I am already in school, should I take some time off to get other
kinds of experience and get more focused on my future, or to pay off
undergraduate school debts, or to travel around before committing to
something else?

5. Am I thinking about graduate school because that's what my
parents want, or because I don't think I can get a job, or because I am
worried about paying off my undergraduate loans, or because I can't
think of anything better to do?

6. If I am already working, do I really need a graduate degree to
enhance my career opportunities?

Part of the investigation should include talking to recent graduates of
programs in which you have an interest in order to see whether their
degree programs led to the career options they envisioned and whether
what they are doing seems really appealing pragmatically as well as
intellectually. If you see yourself as a clinical psychologist, talk to someone in the field (most colleges have alums who are happy to talk to
students) and make sure that being a psychologist is how you want to
spend your days. That means literally asking what the typical day is like.
Also important is asking someone in your potential field whether they
would have gone to graduate school or, instead, taken some other path.
Would an internship at the State Department, for instance, be better
than an MA in international affairs?

Almost without exception a graduate program should be seen as leading to or enhancing a career. All graduate programs are, in a sense, professional programs in that they should make specific employment more possible or more satisfying or more financially rewarding. Students who enter professional or applied programs are already aware of the career that should follow the degree (although they are not always conversant with what daily life is going to be like once on the job), but students who enter, for example, master's programs in the arts and sciences are not always directed toward work goals and are often disappointed at the end of the graduate experience.

Too often graduate school is seen as a safe extension of an educational experience that began, at least, at the age of 5. Students who are clear about what graduate school means usually make better choices about whether or when to enter an advanced degree program.

The question of cost is interwoven into the tapestry of how important, on a very personal level, it is for an individual to get a graduate degree. A young woman recently told me how grim her professors had been about her entering a doctoral program in literature. They gave her all sorts of realistic reasons about why the road to the degree would be a tough and lengthy one, with doubtful prospects for employment at the end. But she had an insatiable passion for the field, and that motivation led her to pursue her goal, despite the warnings. The important point is that she learned about all the good and bad qualities of the field and made an informed decision before going on. She will no doubt also learn as much as she can while in graduate school about what she can do to enhance her future job prospects.

Once a positive, well-informed decision has been made, then cost can be considered. Be sure to look at several factors, including:

1. How much debt have I accumulated from undergraduate school? Would it be more prudent to work for awhile to reduce that debt load or would I be risking my advancement in the field to take time off before entering graduate school? Some science fields, for example, are not enthusiastic about students taking time off unless they do something in the discipline, like work in a laboratory related to the research field.

2. How long is it going to take me to get a degree and what is it going to cost? What will the university contribute in the way of scholarships, fellowships, or assistantships?

3. Can my costs be reduced by going to a state institution?

4. Could I work for a company that would eventually pay my way through a degree program?

5. Will the government pick up the costs of school for a tradeoff of some sort, like going into the military or public health service?

6. Can I make enough money after graduation to pay off a significant number of loans? Is a loan forgiveness program for public sector work available?

7. Will my family help with support?

8. Can I win an external fellowship?

9. Can I work part time and go to school full time, or work full time and go to school part time? (Some programs do not allow part-time matriculation.)

Finding out the answers to these questions is time-consuming but extraordinarily worthwhile. Everyone who approaches graduate school should demystify the financial prospects as thoroughly as possible.

In the end, the answer to whether you should go to graduate school, and whether you can afford it, depends completely on your individual situation. Obviously, there is no universally right answer. There is only your answer.

Tips on Applying to Graduate School

Resources About Graduate Programs

There are four primary types of resources you can tap to determine which graduate programs best suit your interests: publications like *Peterson's Guides*; campus sources such as faculty advisors; people working in the field; and graduate school fairs and forums.

Publications that list graduate programs can usually be found in a variety of places. These materials should be accessible in the campus career center or in the local library or can be purchased or ordered at any bookstore. To order a publication listed in the Further Reading section at the end of this chapter, you can write or call the publisher. These resources are a good start in determining which universities might have the sort of degree program you hope to pursue.

Another good source is **faculty and other advising staff members** who are located on your present campus or, if you know them, on the campus of the school you are considering. Faculty in the field that you want to enter can be especially insightful about which programs will best fit your interests. Faculty keep in close touch with their peers at other universities at annual meetings and have an awareness of who is doing what in the field through publications called journals. They may even be able to give you contacts at other institutions. Many undergraduate schools have faculty or administrators who are designated as pre-professional advisors, especially in pre-law and pre-med. Their advice is very valuable and should be sought out.

As we have already seen, it is also important to talk to **people in the**

field: first to see whether you are choosing the right career; and second, if they are recent graduates, to see whether they they can recommend programs.

A fourth resource is the **fairs and forums.** Some of these are organized by schools either on campus or in regional consortia. Outside organizations such as the Educational Testing Service also arrange regional forums where representatives from a wide variety of graduate schools hand out literature and answer questions.

Graduate Programs as Information Sources

Once you have settled on the names of ten to fifteen programs, you should contact them for literature. If you are interested in information regarding research master's or doctoral degrees, write directly to the departments for literature. If, for example, you are interested in an English MA, then write to the English department and not to the graduate school. Most graduate schools are umbrella organizations that faciliate the admission and matriculation of students in numerous departments; they are good resources about who to contact in departments and will supply important addresses and phone numbers, but the specific program directors invariably know more about their faculty, admissions requirements, financial aid, and so on. Similarly, while it is fine to contact the department administrator for brochures, substantive questions should be addressed to a faculty member, if possible. Almost all programs have a chair or faculty advisor who can answer specific questions, particularly those that involve academic considerations. In some cases it makes sense to talk directly to a faculty member who does research and teaching in the field of interest.

Knowing whom to talk to, of course, is only part of the problem. You also need to find out whether the programs are right for you. What should you know about the programs to which you are applying? There are four basic questions you should ask:

1. Does the program have everything you need in the curriculum or available through the faculty? If a concentration in, let us say, cave archaeology or the Uniform Commercial Code interests you, you should determine that courses and faculty in the field are well established and will still be there when you arrive. More than one student has gone to an institution only to find that the only faculty member with an expertise in African literature, for instance, is on a two year leave.

2. Do you fit the admissions criteria with regard to academic background, grade point average, and test scores? You will want to know how many applicants there are each year and how many of those are accepted. Sometimes this is clear from trade publications and depart-

mental literature; sometimes you must call the program itself. You really do not want to waste time and money applying to a program to which there is absolutely no chance of being admitted.

3. What is the job placement record for recent graduates? What types of positions do they hold and where are they employed?

4. Are currently enrolled students happy in the program?

To How Many Schools Should You Reasonably Apply?

Under normal circumstances the rule is similar to that for undergraduate school. Application should be made to 2 reaches (those where you have only a 25 percent chance of being admitted), 2 reasonables (where your odds are 50–50), and 2 appealing backups (where you cannot possibly conceivably be rejected). You may want to add an extra school in one or more categories, but applying to more than 7 or 8 schools is time consuming as well as expensive. Students in the upper 10 percent of the applicant pool have to be particularly careful not to apply to just the top six to ten programs in the country. When the rejection rate is 95 percent, as it can be in some small, highly prestigious programs, even the most qualified can find themselves being rejected everywhere because the odds of getting in are so low and the competition so spectacular. If a field is very tight and admissions difficult, more than 7 or 8 applications make sense.

Standardized Tests

It is important to determine whether standardized tests are required for application and admission to a program. It is equally important to take the test in time for the application deadline. *Many programs will not even look at an application until the official test scores have arrived.*

Students often wonder if they should take a prep course before the test. First take the practice test included in the application literature and see how it goes. If you feel uncomfortable with the result, either buy a book and prep yourself or go to one of the companies that offer such services and see whether it makes sense to enroll. The commercial courses are expensive, but many people find them worthwhile. Everyone should spend time getting acclimated to the test by reading the directions and working the sections that are provided in the application booklet. No one should enter the test session or sit down to the test computer completely cold.

There is no doubt that standardized tests are important no matter what degree you are pursuing. They are a piece of the admissions puzzle, and while they do not provide a complete picture of the applicant, they are essential to a good evaluation. Educators argue endlessly about how much emphasis, if any, should be put on these exams, but the dependence on them will not change in the near future.

In most cases when programs have large numbers of applicants for a small number of admissions, the propensity is to weed applicants out with test scores and grade point averages. In programs where the admission percentages are higher, standardized tests may not be so important. Some areas of study, English and American literature, for example, will be more concerned with the quality of writing samples than with test scores.

You should determine how important test scores are to programs in which you have an interest. This is easy to do for professional schools, which generally publish ranges, and not always so easy to determine in arts and sciences and engineering programs. Sometimes programs have not really figured it out. In those cases, call a faculty member to determine what he or she thinks is a ballpark range and how much weight test scores carry. In addition, programs may weigh one section of the test more heavily than another (in physics the mathematics score should be more important), and you should be aware of that.

References

All applications ask for references. You want references who know you as someone who will do well in an educational setting and who will write positively. Most graduate schools are not interested in character references. Do not have your pediatrician or pastor write for you unless they know you as a student. (Maybe you are applying to medical school and you did research for your pediatrician.) The best references are those people who have first-hand experience with your academic or professional potential and can attest to those abilities. For an arts and sciences program, a senior faculty member who taught three classes in your major is ideal; for a professional graduate degree program like an MBA program, someone who can testify to the quality of work you have done on the job or in an internship related to your field of interest makes sense. Do not use teaching assistants or adjunct or part-time faculty as references; while it may be unfair, their opinions usually do not carry much weight because of their low status in the department.

Sometimes applicants take time off before they apply. In that case, getting references becomes complicated. Most colleges and universities have an office like a career center that offers a credential file service.

Students can have reference letters put in a file for future use. There are problems attached to this system, however. If you are unclear or change your mind about what sort of program you want to apply to, the letters in the file might not be targeted enough. Letters that are around too long may also be considered too old to be relevant. Consequently, letters in a file can be updated at any time and should be.

The best of all worlds is to get your reference writers to fill out the form provided by the institution and send it directly to the program rather than to rely on credential files. The worry with this system is whether the faculty member will get around to three or four of the schools but forget about the rest. Periodic checking to see if letters have been written can be uncomfortable, but it is necessay.

To help those who write references for you write helpful and timely letters consider doing the following:

1. Write a one-page synopsis about why you want to go to graduate school, what type of degree and program you are interested in, and what your career goals are. This gives the reference writer a sense of your motivation, enthusiasm, and specific direction.

2. Provide the writer with a transcript of your courses and grades and indicate which of those, if any, he or she taught.

3. Provide the writer with copies of papers you have written for his or her course or, if you are getting an industry reference, provide reports you have written or summaries of projects you have undertaken. Items 2 and 3 provide written evidence of your academic potential and can be incorporated into the reference letter.

The worst sort of reference letter is the one in which nothing of substance is said. That usually happens when a referee does know enough about the applicant or does not remember enough. Well-informed references will write a strong, detailed letter that can be attached to the institution's own form.

If you are going to "stop out" for a while, be sure to keep in touch with your mentors. Drop them a postcard if you are far away; call periodically or drop in. Keep yourself current in their minds. I write to my undergraduate mentor once or twice a year, for example, even after almost twenty years, and I am in close contact with my graduate mentor. These are people who should be important to you for your whole life. Serious students need to bond with a faculty member or, in the case of a professional student, a mentor well established in the field who has served as an academic advisor, supervisor, or instructor. If you haven't yet established that contact, do it now. Failure to have established three reference writers who can speak to your potential as a graduate student is a grave mistake.

The Application Essay

Most applicants are given the opportunity to explain why they wish to enter a particular program, what it is about the field that attracts them, and the sort of career goals they have established. An essay can make or break an application. If your grade point average is so-so and your standardized tests are just okay, then the references and the essay become crucial. An essay should demonstrate enthusiasm for the field, motivation to complete a program, and understanding of career goals. Everything should be enhanced by specific information, the more focused and detailed the better. For example, you may have been motivated to enter a master's program in international studies after reading a particular passage in a particular book; that book and passage should be specified. Applicants applying for a PhD program should understand what PhDs in that field do, including the demands of research, publication, and teaching.

Undergraduate applications often require cleverness and a range of diverse interests as keys to success. Graduate applications require the communication of seriousness of purpose, maturity of intellectual thought, and complete focus on the prospective field of study. Do not be cute or clever; only discuss activities that demonstrate a seriousness in pursuing the graduate field. Membership in a history honorary society is a good credential if your chosen area is history; work in a Habitat for Humanity project looks good for a social work program. If you appear too fragmented in your interests, programs assume that you are not focused enough to be devoted to the field or did not spend enough time in the discipline as an undergraduate. There are some instances when leadership in and of itself is a welcome credential, as is the case for professional business school programs, but that information usually appears in other places on the application or references and should not be dwelled upon in the essay.

Deadlines

Earlier is always better. If the admissions are rolling, which means that candidates are considered when the applications comes in, then you must apply early because at some point the openings will be filled and an application filed thereafter will simply be rejected. Programs with set deadlines always have a flurry of mail right before the deadline. This is an opportunity for something to get lost. Get the application in at least two weeks early if possible. Remember that you have little control over many parts of the application, and the more time you leave available, the more complete your application is likely to be. Some departments will not look at an application unless each and every part is there.

Be sure to call periodically to check that everything has arrived. Some programs are wonderful and send status cards to applicants. Others are not so wonderful. So despite the fact that you may make yourself a "nudge," it is better to be sure everything is there yourself. Do not depend upon anyone else.

Acceptances and Rejections

If you are offered acceptances by several appealing programs and are planning on relocating for three or more years, be sure to visit your first choice, at least. When visiting, talk to students and see how they like the program and the faculty. Get a sense of how students are regarded. Some institutions, unfortunately, hold the student population in low esteem and, as a result, the placement services may be second-rate, as may other items like health insurance and other benefits. Find out how successful graduates are at finding suitable jobs. Talk to faculty in your area of interest to make sure they are going to be around for awhile and how interested they seem in helping students. If the vibes are bad, visit your second choice. This advice is especially true for applicants to research doctoral programs where the time to degree ranges from five to eight years.

What If You Are Rejected by Every School?

Occasionally an applicant is rejected by every program. If you submitted carefully constructed and complete applications, two things are likely to be the cause. First, the schools selected for application may all have been reaches. If this is the case, then the solution is to visit program resources again and be more realistic in picking institutions where admission is feasible. The second likely cause is an unusually high application pool. During the early 1990s, when unemployment was high, a record number of undergraduates applied to graduate programs. This phenomenon raised admission standards, and programs became much more selective than previously. Keep tuned to all the factors that affect applicant pools, especially employment in general as well as within the field. During large application pool years try applying to more schools than normal and setting your sights a little lower to compensate for tight admissions. Seriously consider strengthening the application, for instance, by taking a graduate class in the field, and reapplying. Calling the program and asking why you were rejected may or may not be productive, but it is worth a try.

During the spring semester of your junior year in college or, for those not in school, the spring before applying to graduate school (roughly eighteen months before anticipated enrollment), you should investigate external funding possibilities. Those options are the subject of Chapter 2.

Further Reading

Directory of Graduate Programs. Princeton, NJ: Educational Testing Service. Annual.

Gourman, Jack. *The Gourman Report: A Rating of Graduate and Professional Programs in American and International Universities.* Sixth edition. Los Angeles: National Education Standards, 1993.

Graduate School and You: A Guide for Prospective Graduate Students. Washington, DC: Council of Graduate Schools, 1994.

Peterson's: An Overview, Graduate and Professional Programs. Princeton, NJ: Peterson's Guides. Annual.

Peterson's Guides to Graduate Study. Princeton, NJ: Peterson's Guides.
   Humanities and Social Sciences
   Biological and Agricultural Sciences
   Physical Sciences and Mathematics
   Engineering and Applied Sciences
   Business, Education, Health, and Law

Chapter 2
External Funding

Institutional or internal funding is the financial aid offered to applicants or enrolled students by or through the university to which they are applying or in which they are enrolled. In Chapter 1 we discussed the various forms of institutional funding in detail.

Funds that come to a student or applicant from outside their university are called external funds and include the money that comes from government agencies, private industry, and not-for-profit foundations. There are times when the distinctions are not very clear. Sometimes a university or a department will apply to an external source for money that it will then offer to qualified applicants or enrolled students as institutional sources. The federal Department of Education, for example, offers what we call *training grants* to limited disciplines (biology, chemistry, engineering, foreign languages, mathematics, and physics) through a program called Graduate Assistance in the Area of National Need so that departments can recruit U.S. students into their programs. The programs then support their students with Department of Education monies. While financial resources of this type could be considered a form of external funds, in this book we treat them as institutional or internal funds, because they are awarded to candidates by the institution rather than by the funding agency.

For our purposes, *external funds* are those grants or fellowships that require an applicant or enrolled student to submit an application directly to the outside agency in order to access the resources. While the institution with which the applicant or enrolled student is affiliated may be very helpful in facilitating the process, such as with Rhodes or Fulbright Fellowships, the application process takes place between the individual and the funding agency.

With a few minor exceptions, the rest of this book will deal with external funding opportunities, how to find out about them, and how to apply for them. It is important to state from the outset that most of the funding the average graduate student receives is institutional. The usual PhD graduate enters the program with an internally funded fellowship, teaching assistantship, or research assistantship. While enrolled, he or she may get a small external grant or dissertation fellowship, particularly in the sciences or social sciences. But the ratio of institutional to external dollars for the average doctoral student would run at least 20 to 1 or higher. The credentials of the student, the quality of his or her program, and the amount of money available in the field, plus the aggressiveness of the university in encouraging students to apply for external funding, determines the ratio.

There are two notable exceptions to the radio rule. The first is in the area of minority funding for both master's and doctoral programs. Ever-increasing amounts of government and private sector money are being funneled to primarily African American and Hispanic applicants and students. People in these two minority categories should be especially alert for these opportunities.

The second is in funding to travel and do research or study abroad. In this area particularly, money is readily available. Almost everyone with a research project of any merit should be able to find money from government or private agencies to support all or part of the project. For example, my son received money from the Explorers Club to do field archaeology in Greece when he was a sophomore in college. The funds covered almost 50 percent of his expenses.

These exceptions aside, if external money is not as accessible as internal funding, why bother to apply for outside money at all? First, entering students who receive portable training grant fellowships, like those offered by the National Science Foundation or the Department of Education's Javits Fellowships, find that they can virtually pick their program. While external funding is not an absolute admissions guarantee, most programs would not turn away a student with three or four full years of external support. Students with those same fellowships are usually guaranteed additional institutional funding once their external fellowships are exhausted.

Winning an external award is also an important credential that helps in securing more external funding and can be highly regarded on a resume. For those in certain doctoral programs such as anthropology that require continuous and extensive field research, finding external money is a way of life and being good at getting it can guarantee a fruitful short- and long-term career. The same can be said for the sciences. The key to success in the academic laboratory sciences is the ability to keep winning outside funds. A research chemist at a large university, for example, who cannot secure significant numbers of grants will find it difficult to run a productive laboratory.

The final reason for applying outside the university system for grants and fellowships relates to advanced doctoral students. Nothing crystallizes the dissertation project more than writing a grant application. This is true even when a proposal has been written for the department. The demands of a grant proposal, especially those written sometime after constructing a dissertation proposal, can be an enormous help in further defining the project. In addition, it can bring a student back to a dissertation when the work trail has grown cold and infuse new enthusiasm into the research.

The key to determining whether applying for external funds makes sense is first to establish whether there are funds available in the field. In medicine, for example, there is not much available short of those payback/loan forgiveness opportunities discussed earlier for applicants interested in MD degrees. But for those seeking a combined MD/PhD the internal and external funding odds get dramatically better. Another important factor is expectations in the field, and whether the department or institution expects students to seek external funding.

Doctoral students in every field should apply for external support of some sort while in graduate school. There is external money for all types of research projects. Humanists may be put off by this idea and will certainly find fewer opportunities. Their awards, aside from study/research abroad, will also yield fewer dollars than those available to social and natural scientists, yet travel grants to libraries and special collections and small, field specific research grants abound and should be pursued. In my own case, in the improbable field of social/cultural history, I was able to apply for and receive a sizable state research grant to study the architecture of a rural county. My eventual dissertation topic involved the WPA and a particular architectural project and so the year studying building styles was very helpful both academically and financially.

The first step in applying for outside funding is to figure out what is available in your specific degree field. Even if you are expected routinely to apply for particular outside funds, you also must determine whether you have the right credentials for a successful application. Good test scores and a high grade point average may be essential for some fellowships, while arresting research projects and strong faculty support are the key to others. Being under-represented in your field, which can mean all sorts of things but especially refers to minorities and women, is another important credential for some funding.

Under circumstances where student-generated external funding ap-

plications are routine or when virtually all faculty in an area are supporting their research through outside funding, getting the credentials
for successful applications becomes crucial. If you find faculty enthusiasm for your project waning and thus external awards elusive, you
need to give serious consideration to finding a more engaging project
or, as a last resort, leaving the discipline. Reevaluating your suitability
for your field of study is a drastic step, but failure to get funding when
academic survival depends on it means that your future does not bode
well. Anthropologists, for example, who want to do field research
simply *must* find a benefactor outside the university in order to continue to do their work.

Resources for Funding External Grants and Fellowships

Many resources are geared toward helping students and applicants
find money for graduate study and research. The best, most reliable,
and most current information is always found on the agency brochure
and application form. But other resources are also available to help you
find funding sources that are right for you.

Publications

The Further Reading section at the end of this chapter lists a fair
number of books published nationally. Some are directed to particular
populations (e.g., women, minorities, artists, scientists) or to specific
fields (e.g., history, philosophy). A few resources give comprehensive
information; most give a cursory description of the grant or fellowship
and supply an address and phone number as well. The typical listing
will give you enough information to tell whether the grant is relevant to
your interests.

If you are on a campus, good comprehensive books, such as *Peterson's
Grants for Graduate Students*, can usually be found in one of several
places. The main academic library is usually a good place to start. If
there is a career center or career planning and placement office with a
library, they may have books on external funding as well. Large universities with graduate schools often keep these resources in the graduate
school office or the staff may know where to find them. They may also
be found in the undergraduate administrative offices. Information on
special funding sources like study abroad grants and fellowship books
may be located in the international studies or study abroad office.
Many of the research universities, such as the University of California
at Los Angeles, Indiana University at Bloomington, and Washington
University in St. Louis, make an effort to centralize external funding

information and make it readily accessible to undergraduate and graduate students. Numerous schools also produce their own grant guides, which highlight external fellowships and research grants that might be of particular interest to their student body. Harvard University puts out a booklet for students that is available in the career planning offices while the graduate division at UCLA produces a publication for graduate students.

If you do not have access to a campus or cannot find printed resources there, a search of the local public library might be fruitful, especially in larger metropolitan areas.

An important source about federal government funding that should be available in most university and public libraries is the *Catalog of Federal Domestic Assistance*. This mammoth volume lists every funding opportunity offered through the various agencies of the federal government. It is updated once a year. The most current listing for federal grants is the daily *Federal Register*, but the *Catalog* is sufficiently current and comprehensive for most student needs. The indexing is superb, and in most cases the grant descriptions give sample titles of the most recently funded research. This is a fine resource for students looking for research money in the sciences and social sciences.

Another especially good place to look for financial resources is in a publication entitled the *Encyclopedia of Associations*. This multivolume work can usually be found in the reference section of the library. Publications such as the *Peterson's Guides* lists the largest, most national sources; the *Encyclopedia of Associations* is a fine source for some of the smaller, less nationally known grants and fellowships either for tuition assistance or to support research. Among other things, it lists ethnic organizations that offer support to students within their particular group. International students from China, for example, might find a Chinese-American association that has funding available for students who are from China or are Chinese Americans. The encyclopedia also lists small scientific organizations that may support specific field research with small grants.

Most states have some organization that publishes books on state or regional foundations. Missouri, for example, had the *Corporate Funders Operating in Missouri* and the *Directory of Missouri Foundations*. The corporate and not-for-profit organizations that are found in state and regional resources tend to be most interested in funding research proposals in the fields of education, social welfare, and health care, especially if research is done at the local level or if the student is interested in particular state communities.

State agencies are also an important potential source of research money, especially in the social sciences. Most states put out a book of some sort that summarizes the missions of its various agencies and, in some cases, the research money that is available. The secretary of state's office is usually the best place to call or visit to find out whether such a book or pamphlet is published or, if not, where the information is located. The state library may also house such data.

Computerized Searching

In recent years, several institutions and organizations have established funding information databases. The most notable of these are at Stanford and the University of Illinois. Other colleges, universities, and organizations can access these databases through a computerized network. Often students can take advantage of these subscriptions to have a computer funding search done. This is a valuable resource for students doing research. The program at Indiana University, for example, helps nearly 1,000 students a year search for external funding. Other schools like Washington University in St. Louis have a small staff who search several computer databases for close to 100 students per year. It is worthwhile checking with your university library reference section to see if a computer funding search is possible, especially for advanced graduate students.

You should never rely solely on the computer search. Start with printed resources first and then have a computer search run. The typical computer search printout is usually equal in descriptiveness to book resources. Printed books offer the searcher a chance to browse through lots of sections and try various indexing approaches that simply are not available through computer searching, since you must usually rely on someone else to run the computer search and that person may use limited searching strings and come up with limited results.

Other Information Sources

Two other important funding information sources are departmental faculty and advanced graduate students. In departments where researchers are routinely applying for outside money, faculty are a significant fount of information. This is especially true for faculty who have recently finished their graduate studies and secured external funding during their graduate or postdoctoral years. More senior faculty may be somewhat removed from the days of writing small, start-up funding proposals, but they unfailingly have important contacts with funding agencies.

Advisement offices, libraries, or departments may also have information about funding. Graduate students or postdocs who have recently gotten external support are also knowledgeable advisors about what works on an application. Students should pressure departments to hold regular workshops on finding funding sources and grant proposal writing and to maintain files with copies of successful student applications.

Some campuses have administrators who spend a lot of time helping students find funding resources and also help with application writing. These people are usually found in the graduate division, school or the research office, the undergraduate college and sometimes in the library or career center.

Up-to-Date Information

The absolutely most current as well as comprehensive information is found in the annually published brochures and applications that are produced by the funding agencies themselves. Anything found in trade publications is by definition one or two years out of date. The most serious consequence of out-of-date information is the application deadline. Agencies, especially those connected with federal or state governments, have frequent deadline changes. Even computer databases are not always as current as one might imagine regarding the most recent information on deadlines. After you determine which funding resources are most appealing, it is important to call or write the agencies and get confirmation that the grant or fellowship is still available and what the current deadline is.

Some agencies change their topic interest from time to time and a call seeking advice on what their focus is can be very important. This is, again, especially true with the federal and state governmental agencies, especially in the health care and social welfare fields. AIDS research grants in medicine and social welfare services, for example, are much more prevalent than they once were.

Advisors often tell students, especially those seeking research project money, that once they have gotten a list of funding resources, have written to the agencies, and have received applications, they should call any agency that is vague about where their current funding interests lie. As we will see later, some agencies are clear about what topics they fund and some are specific about the field but vague about topics. The National Science Foundation (NSF), for example, funds dissertation research in behavioral and social sciences as well as non-medical biological disciplines, but it may find specific areas of interest within the fields more attractive at one moment than another. For example, a call to the anthropology area at NSF by a faculty mentor of the doctoral student can establish what is considered fundable and help the applicant either to better focus the application or to consider not applying at all. If a call indicates that a research topic is not fundable, you have saved lots of time and energy.

If the deadline is coming up and an application is not readily available, or if the deadline is past, you need to make an immediate phone call to the funding source. Grants and fellowships for which there are fewer applications often have flexible deadlines; so before you give up, or spend hours of fruitless work, you should get assurance that applications are no longer being accepted.

Grant and Fellowship Applications

For the more common grants and fellowships, applications should be available somewhere on campus. Portable fellowship applications such as those from the National Science Foundation, the Department of Education, or the Department of Defense are always sent to colleges and universities and may be found in the undergraduate or graduate administrative offices, the research office, the library, or the career center. However, always be sure to check applications you get from these sources to make sure they are current.

Some outside competitions must be applied for through the college or university. This is true for the Rhodes, Marshall, Churchill, Fulbright, and Fulbright-Hays Fellowships, and for others as well. Again, the undergraduate or graduate administrative offices will know who orchestrates these competitions.

If you are not affiliated with a college or university, or if applications are not readily available on campus, call or write to the agency.

Types of External Funding

In order to save time and trouble in applying for external funds, it helps to understand the different kinds of funding available. This section gives concise descriptions of types of external funding. Subsequent chapters will enhance the information below with application hints and descriptions of specific funding opportunities.

Individual Fellowships

The National Science Foundation, Mellon, Jacob Javits, Howard Hughes, GEM, and National Hispanic Graduate Fellowships are just a few examples of grants for which senior undergraduates and first-year graduate students may apply. They usually include money for tuition and a stipend allowance. In most cases they may be used at any accredited institution, which means they are portable. Multiple years of support are typically the rule with these awards.

Funding for Study or Research Abroad

Students are generally interested in study or research abroad at three points of their academic careers. The first is during their undergraduate years when there is interest in either a summer program or one or two semesters in the junior year. External funding opportunities do exist for this category as exemplified by the previously mentioned description of the summer funding my son received to do field archaeology in Greece during his sophomore year. The United States Information Agency, which directs the various Fulbright programs, has also gotten more interested in sending students to foreign countries during the later years of high school and the middle years of college.

Undergraduate students are also very interested in pursuing study/ research programs the year following graduation. If you have these interests, you should start looking at Fulbright, Rotary, Rhodes, Marshall, Churchill, and other programs during the spring semester of your junior year.

Early investigation into the Rotary and Fulbright fellowships is critical. Almost all colleges and universities have information about these programs. The potential for getting funded is very good for students with sufficient language skills, interesting study plans or research projects, and connections abroad. While exceptional academic credentials are required for the Rhodes, Marshall, and Churchill programs, this is not as true for the Rotary or Fulbright where good language skills, worthy projects, and ambassadorial potential can be even more important.

Students engaged in many areas of graduate study are also interested in study or research abroad and opportunities are abundant.

Students with the qualifications to go to school or conduct research in a foreign country should actively pursue fellowship and grant opportunities because the chances of getting partial or full financial support are very good.

Small Research Grants

Small research grants are available to students at any level in all programs. While they are more likely to be found in arts and sciences programs, it is not impossible to receive them in other fields. They fall into three categories.

The first is the small exploratory grant, which is meant to encourage the development of ideas. The research project is usually in the embryonic stages and the money goes to support—for example, a preliminary survey or elemental laboratory or field work.

The second type of small grant is meant to contribute to on-going research. In some cases these funds can keep a project going or aid in writing up the final project.

The third type of small grant is highly focused on a subject area. The Woodrow Wilson Foundation administers a grant specifically for research about women. Similar kinds of grants are offered by disciplinary organizations like the American Historical Association. Small travel grants to view holdings are plentiful. The presidential libraries, for instance, offer many small grants to faculty and students as an incentive to visit their facilities and do research. Many libraries with special collections also have readily available travel grants for worthy projects.

Students at all levels, from undergraduate to graduate, should be on the lookout for these opportunities.

In-Residence Study or Research Funding

Certain institutions and federal agencies offer students an opportunity to go to a facility other than their own to do specialized training or research. The Smithsonian Institution has numerous such situations available to students at all levels. Students in art history can apply for a myriad of paid internships. Artists can pursue writing, composing, and painting in special residencies. Sometimes in-residence fellowships are given by institutions located abroad.

Large Research Grants

Everything said for small research grants applies to large grants. Students who are most likely to be eligible for grants in this category are fairly advanced in their research. Usually they are at the final stages of graduate work and engaged in the research or writing of a final project, thesis, or dissertation. Students in the social sciences and sciences are the most likely to be interested in large grant opportunities.

Dissertation Fellowships

Foundations and agencies set aside money specifically to fund dissertation research and/or writing. The National Science Foundation offers a dissertation grant to students in the sciences and social sciences, and the National Endowment for the Humanities offers a similar opportunity to doctoral students in the humanities and related social sciences. Grants of this nature have a large range of purposes, including support for living expenses while doing research and writing domestically or even abroad; the Fulbright-Hays Dissertation Fellowship, for example, provides funding for area studies outside of the United States. Money is also available to cover expenses incurred in research, including the purchase of a special microscope or computer, the copying and mailing of surveys, or the rental of recording or photography equipment.

Dissertation grants and fellowships may be offered to large groups of people with little regard to topic. The American Association of University Women fellowships, for example, are accessible to women in almost any field. Dissertation funding may support work in specific fields (for example, the American Council of Learned Societies Eastern European Studies Grant) or on specific topics (for example, the Spencer Foundation Dissertation Fellowship in education).

Grants and Fellowships for Underrepresented and Specially Defined Groups

Every year more and more money is made available for underrepresented and specialty groups of people. Such grants might go to such general groups as African Americans, Hispanics, or Native Americans or such specific groups as women in science. While these four groups are most highly targeted, this is by no means an exclusive list. Awards are given, for example, to women whose mothers are members of P.E.O., a midwestern organization.

Every type of grant and fellowship is available in this category. The National Science Foundation training fellowships set aside support for minorities and women, for example.

Postdoctoral Fellowships

In recent years, increasing numbers of students have received their degrees and then gone on to training positions called postdoctorates. Postdocs are transitional periods wedged between the graduate and permanent placement years. People holding postdocs often complain that they are neither fish nor fowl because they are not privy to the institutional services offered to graduate students while at the same time they lack the clout and security of faculty. Commonly found in the sciences for many years, such awards have recently become more prevalent in the social sciences and humanities.

A postdoctoral position can serve several functions. The first purpose is educational. Scientists often need to spend several years after graduate school to complete important research or hone laboratory techniques. In the applied social sciences, postdocs offer a chance to practice skills learned at the graduate level. In the humanities, as well as other disciplines, a postdoc may become the place where a graduate can continue on-going research or enhance his or her credentials by publishing an article or a book, or it can be a holding position in a tight job market.

Departmental Training Grants

While departmental training grants are not external grants by this book's definition, they are funds about which potential applicants should be aware. As we have seen, money to support students may be made available to departments by outside funding agencies including the National Institutes of Health, the Department of Education, and the National Science Foundation, as well as corporations such as Merck and McDonnell Douglas. Departments apply to these organizations and, if they are successful, can receive as much as $5 million a year, which goes to students in the way of stipends and tuition scholarships.

The Department of Education gives departments up to $300,000 a year for individual academic programs in the fields of biology, chemistry, engineering, foreign languages, mathematics, and physics. Since departments that have lots of training grant money may take more students, getting in may be easier and receiving perpetual funding more likely. Sometimes a university will advertise that it has training grants for applicants. Applicants should be sure to ask any program in which they have an interest whether training grant money is plentiful and how long enrolled students can expect to be funded from these resources.

Grant and Fellowship Application Hints

The chapters that follow will give application hints that relate to specific grant types. Below are general hints about beginning the application process and writing proposals. Be sure to read this section first before going on to the specific type of grant that is of interest.

General Advice

1. **Start early.** This is true for any grant or fellowship but especially true for research and study abroad opportunities, since funds are usually not awarded until at least ten to fifteen months after the ap-

plication is filed. This is particularly the case with funding that cover stipends to support room and board for a year or more either in the United States or abroad. Smaller grants usually have deadlines three to six months prior to initiation of the grant spending period. The important principle is to investigate research opportunities well in advance so that you do not miss crucial deadlines.

2. **Be sure to consult knowledgeable people on campus about funding.** Be careful to seek out everyone including faculty, other graduate students, and administrators who work regularly with funding information. Someone will have good information about where to look for outside money or can indicate who else on campus has more information.

3. **Be persistent.** Too often students give up quickly when information about grants is not easy to find or when their application is rejected. Students looking for research money, especially, should keep hunting for opportunities and keep applying. There are times, however, when reason should win out over persistence. If you are in the last stages of writing your thesis or dissertation, for example, and waiting would unnecessarily defer attainment of your degree, it is probably smarter to take out a loan to cover expenses rather than apply for a grant that may not come through for 10 months.

4. **Do not count on one application.** There are some exceptions to this rule but in general the more applications you file, the better the odds are that you will win an award. Write as many as feasible.

5. **Be sure your credentials, study plan, or project fit the agency's criteria.** It is important to read the application sections on eligibility and the field focus requirements very carefully. Permanent residents should be particularly careful; the federal government is especially inconsistent about including or excluding this group. Research projects should fit very closely to agency interests and parameters.

6. **Deadlines are sometimes flexible.** The more applications there are for a grant or fellowship, the less flexible the deadline is likely to be. A surprising number of agencies issuing research grants will bend a deadline rule if the date has not been missed by more than a week or two. When in doubt, have a faculty mentor or university administrator call the organization to inquire about and possibly influence deadline flexibility.

7. **If you are confused, call the funding agency.** There are times when a brochure or application leaves many questions unanswered. Statements of eligibility are not always clear, and agency interests may be hazy or shifting. You do not want to waste your time and energy applying for a grant that is out of reach. Most organizations are very

helpful in clarifying their aims since they prefer to receive applications that are right on target with agency interests.

8. **Feel free to send additional materials after you have submitted your application.** There is usually a time between the deadline and committee review when applications are being sorted and scored. Most organizations will add new pieces of information to an application within this period. If additions significantly strengthen an application, be sure to forward them for inclusion. Written confirmation of contacts abroad, for example, can be crucial to the success of a Fulbright or Fulbright-Hays application. Timing is everything, since the new information must arrive before review begins. If you are in doubt about that window of opportunity, call the agency.

9. **Do not be discouraged by rejection.** Students often give up after the first rejection. Instead, try to figure out what the weakness was and correct it. This is particularly true for research grants. Was your methodology unclear? Did you not follow the directions closely enough? Could your faculty support have been stronger? Would another agency be more interested in the work? Could the budget be reworked? Sometimes agencies will return the proposal with an evaluation, but usually they will not. Faculty and administrators can be helpful in criticizing and suggesting solutions to problems. A lot of money awarded by the federal government is tied to the availability of funds at any given time and amounts accessible can vary wildly from year to year. Resubmission in less lean years may be the simple solution to rejection. Students looking for dissertation support should consider reapplying to the same agency. As research progresses and the holes that were present in the beginning are filled, the project becomes more attractive and promising to funding organizations. One student I know succeeded in winning a nationally prominent dissertation fellowship on the third try.

10. **Try to find out the ratio of applications to awards.** This information gives a realistic picture of the probability of winning and can help you decide whether or not to apply. Let's say that you are thinking about applying for a national fellowship that pays tuition and stipend support. If there are 4,000 applications for 60 grants, it is logical to assume that only students with the highest standardized test score, grade point averages, and recommendations will be funded. If you have those credentials, then an application makes sense. Some applications fall into a gray zone where it is not so apparent statistically whether application is logical. When in doubt, apply.

11. **Follow directions scrupulously.** The biggest mistake applicants make is not to follow directions. If an agency wants methodology first, put it first. Most reviewers are given a list of evaluation criteria that

reflect application directions. Beside each criterion is a numerical value. If methodology is worth 5 points and if the reviewer has to search for methodology or it is not well explained, then those 5 points are lost. And so it goes throughout the entire review. A proposal is no place for subtle nuances that might be missed. If the application enumerates the criteria under a particular requirement, your response to that requirement should be similarly numbered and titled. If the application wants to know whether "(iv) *The applicant has made preparations to establish research contacts and affiliations abroad*," it makes sense in your application proposal to have a section called "(iv) Contacts and Affiliations Abroad."[1]

Following directions carefully dramatically improves your chances of winning. Reviewers are generally overworked and are functioning within a very short time frame. If a reviewer has to hunt for the answers in your application when she or he is reading 100 applications in 5 days, the application will not make a good impression.

Proposal Writing Advice

1. **Use the funding agency's terminology.** A proposal sounds like it fits a funding agency's criteria if their words (gotten either from the brochure or from the application) are appropriately replicated in the proposal. Using the same terminology is tantamount both substantively and psychologically to responding directly to application critera or agency mission.

2. **Do not use excessive disciplinary jargon; write clearly and simply.** Many applications are reviewed by people in related fields or disciplines. Excessive jargon may be unrecognizable and therefore confusing and end up costing review points. An anthropology Fulbright applicant who keeps referring to the animals she or he is proposing to study by their Latin names would be well advised to call them "monkeys" once in awhile to make the proposal more understandable to the non-physical anthropology readers who will surely be evaluating it.

3. **Avoid excessive verbiage.** Getting to the point in a clear, concise, and comprehensive manner will be heartily appreciated by agencies and reviewers.

4. **Put the research you describe within the context of the entire project.** If you are seeking funding to support part but not all of a project. It is important that the part be framed within the context of the

---

1. This example is taken from the U.S. Department of Education Application for Fulbright-Hays Training Grants, 1993, p. 12.

entire project so that reviewers can judge how crucial it is to the plan and better understand the overall significant of the project.

5. **Indicate the significance of why you want funding.** In the case of fellowships to support a graduate school career, a description of career goals assuring the agency that you want to do serious research or contribute to the betterment of society is important. For those requesting money for research, it is crucial to present a project that will make a contribution to the field.

6. **Work closely with a campus advisor or faculty mentor when writing the proposal.** If you are applying for a campus-administered grant or fellowship like a Fulbright, pay close attention to what the administrator says and have her or him review at least one draft of the proposal before completing the final version. If you are engaged in research, your faculty mentor is the best critic and his or her advice should be heeded. Most research projects have no chance if they lack faculty enthusiasm, and the best way to ensure that fervor is to work closely with your advisor.

7. **Be willing to redraft a proposal three or four times.** Patience and persistence will help produce an effective document.

8. **Have other people read the proposal for content, style, and typos.** The faculty or administrative advisor should read your proposal for content. If avoiding disciplinary jargon is crucial, have someone from another field evaluate the clarity of style. Have a person you really trust as a stickler for detail and language structure read it for language structure and typos.

9. **Be willing to reorganize the proposal to fit different applications.** There is a propensity to want to make one proposal fit all grant applications because it is easier. This is a terrible mistake. An agency must recognize the project as something they could own, and so it must be described in their terms and according to their standards. Reworking a project description is absolutely worth the effort.

10. **If there is a weakness in the application of any sort, address it.** Maybe a bad grade shows up on a transcript. Explain what happened; do not dwell on it but clarify the problem. Maybe you lack language skills. Explain how this weakness can be or is being remedied. Anything that might cause concern should be demystified.

11. **Never sound tentative.** Do not use phrases like "I might be interested in . . . ," "I think it is possible that . . . ," or "there is a good chance that. . . ." These words suggest lack of confidence, confusion about direction, and indecisiveness.

12. **Be crystal clear about methodology.** Methodology is a plan of action, your approach to a problem or area of study. It is the structure that you will follow to get things done. For a fellowship applicant, it

indicates how the graduate years will be structured (types of classes, specific field selection, possible research interests). For a student who intends to do research abroad, methodology can include the steps it will take to gather information, where that information is to be found, and so on. Methodology should reflect acceptable practices in the field. Every application requires an explanation of method even if the directions do not demand it in so many words.

Getting Good References

1. **References should almost always be written by people who can attest to your academic promise or ability.** The application will usually indicate the most appropriate referees. In most cases this means faculty, although there are instances when an expert from outside academe, like the head of a laboratory at a corporation doing field-related research, is an acceptable choice. Most agencies are not interested in character references.

When using faculty references try to utilize full-time people with faculty ranks ranging from assistant to full professor. Their opinions carry more weight than those of part-time faculty, postdocs, or teaching assistants. Teaching assistants, especially, lack credibility because they are in training and are viewed as short on the experience needed to be able to judge other people's academic prospects. Part-time instructors (often called adjuncts) are not usually the best option unless they are famous in the field.

2. **A reference should know the applicant and be willing to write supportively and enthusiastically.** Weak or negative references will kill a proposal's prospects. Lukewarm praise is not much good either. Be sure to ask if a referee is willing to write positively. If not, find someone else who will.

3. **Give referees plenty of advance notice.** People who write references for grant or graduate school applications are usually besieged with requests, especially in the late fall. If you can give referees two or three weeks to get a letter constructed and sent, the odds are the letter will be better.

4. **Give referees enough written information upon which to base the reference.** Be sure to supply a copy of the proposal and a résumé or curriculum vitae. Undergraduates applying for Fulbright, Rhodes, and other national fellowships should be sure to make a list of every course taken with the referee, the grades in those courses, and a copy of a significant paper written for the referee. Be sure the referee understands why winning the grant is important. The more written

material a referee has, the better the reference and the sooner the letter will be written.

5. **Check periodically to make sure the reference has been written.** Faculty, especially, are notoriously absent-minded. While nudging is a delicate issue and one must be careful not to become a nuisance, it is important to remain visible so that the letter of reference does not get shoved to the back burner. Some students work through departmental administrators, who often have greater license to prod, while others leave notes. If you are away from campus, a well-timed phone call or a written note can be effective. The squeaky wheel concept works.

Chapters 1 and 2 have served to introduce the worlds of graduate school and internal and external funding. They have offered advice to facilitate the selection of a graduate program and construction of applications for external grants and fellowships. The rest of this book will target specific funding opportunities. Although a limited number of grants and fellowships will be discussed, the information offered can be applied to other support opportunities.

Further Reading

Blum, Laurie. *Free Money for Graduate School.* New York: Henry Holt, 1993.

Cassidy, Daniel. *The Graduate Scholarship Directory.* Third edition. National Scholarship Research Service. Englewood Cliffs, NJ: Career Press, 1993.

Educational Grants for Minority Students: A Selected Listing of Associations, Foundations, Funds. Champaign-Urbana: Compiled by the University of Illinois Graduate College, Minority Student Affairs Office, 1989.

Grants for Graduate and Postdoctoral Study. University of Massachusetts at Amherst. Princeton, NJ: Peterson's Guides, Inc. 1994.

McWade, Patricia. *Financing Graduate School.* Princeton, NJ: Peterson's Guides, 1992.

Muto, Lisa M. and Kristine Forsgaid. *The Harvard College Guide to Grants.* Cambridge, MA: Harvard University Office of Career Services, 1991.

Schlachter, Gail Ann. *Directory of Financial Aids for Women.* San Carlos, CA: Reference Service Press, 1993.

Schlachter, Gail Ann and David R. Webber. *Directory of Financial Aids for Minorities.* San Carlos, CA: Reference Service Press, 1993.

Weeg, Carol, ed. *Funding for U.S. Study: A Guide for Foreign Nationals.* New York: Institutional for International Education, 1990.

Chapter 3
Individual Fellowships

This chapter presents general information and application writing advice for all the individual training fellowships for which a student may apply. It also describes in detail certain specific fellowship opportunities, namely:

1. Department of Defense Acquisition Scholarships
2. Department of Defense Graduate Fellowships
3. Ford Foundation Predoctoral Fellowships for Minorities
4. GEM Fellowship Program
5. Howard Hughes Predoctoral Fellowships in the Biological Sciences
6. Indian Education Fellowship Program
7. Jacob K. Javits Fellowships for the Arts, Humanities, and Social Sciences
8. Mellon Fellowships in Humanistic Studies
9. National Hispanic Scholarships
10. National Science Foundation Graduate Fellowships in the Sciences, Social Sciences, and Engineering and National Science Foundation Minority Fellowships and Women in Engineering Awards
11. National Security Education Fellowships for Foreign Language and Area Studies

Fellowships in this section are of interest to: Junior and senior undergraduates; first- through fifth-year graduate students.
Fields funded by one or more of these fellowships: Most fields.
Degree programs funded by these fellowships: Master's and doctoral.

General Information

Grants that provide money to pay tuition costs and fees and offer stipends for living expenses, books, and supplies for the first years of graduate education are called *training fellowships.* Some agencies provide funds to universities to distribute to students, others require that individual student applications be sent directly to the funding organization. The first type of fellowship was discussed in Chapter 1. This chapter discusses fellowships awarded through direct application.

Undoubtedly the greatest volume of graduate student support money is offered as training fellowships. Every year the National Science Foundation alone funds 900 to 1,000 new three-year awards, each worth $22,500 per year—an annual outlay of $22,500,000 just for new fellowships. Millions more is spent to support continuing fellows, a significant amount of money to engineering, science, and social science graduate education.

The federal government is the single greatest provider of training fellowship money, but not the only source. Private organizations also support students in the first years of their programs, although only a limited number award more than a few grants per year.

If you want to apply for any of the training fellowships described in this chapter, you should remember to *obtain the most current and accurate information directly from the funding agency.* Between the writing and publication of this book, deadlines, stipend amounts, and applicant criteria may have changed. The most important point of this book is to make you aware of fellowships, help you understand how each fellowship is constructed and to what population it is targeted, provide you with the most recent agency address and telephone number, and give you advice about how to approach the application. It is not to be used as a definitive source of information on any specific resource.

General Application Advice

1. **Read and reread the application again and again from beginning to end.** Understand the underlying philosophy of why the fellowship was created, try to visualize what sort of student the organization wants to support, be clear on the application requirements, decipher the funding potential, be aware of any paybacks.

2. **If something is not clear on the application, find someone on campus to answer your questions or call the agency.** Many applications leave significant areas murky. Administrators and faculty on campus who have worked with the agency are good sources for quick answers. Agencies offer the most reliable answers about the nuts and bolts

of the application process such as when awards will be announced, how funding is arranged once an award is made, if it is possible to defer an award for a year, and so on.

3. **Agencies are looking for academically focused individuals who they believe will end up in careers in which they will contribute to the betterment of the discipline and society.** The Jacob Javits Fellowship, for example, is designed to draw the brightest students into academic research and teaching in humanities, social sciences, and the arts.

Therefore, when writing the proposal statement be as academically knowledgeable and focused as possible. Applications to undergraduate school, as we have seen, often encourage cleverness or diversity of interest. The opposite is true in this case. Judges will be more convinced that you are motivated and enthusiastic about your field and committed to completing your degree if you demonstrate a solid intellectual grounding in the field and, in the best of worlds, can even demonstrate a subfield expertise. This is not always easy for senior students, who may have had no more than two years of study in a field. Agencies are simply trying, at the application stage, to predict which applicants have been the most motivated in their studies and are likely to remain enthusiastic. Accessing an applicant's knowledge base is one way of predicting potential success.

Each application will indicate the fellowship's purpose. The Department of Defense states in the beginning of its 1994–1995 Graduate Fellowship application that it is "committed to increasing the number and quality of our Nation's scientists and engineers. Toward that end, the DoD annually supports approximately 8,000 graduate students in fields important to national defense needs." Nothing could be more clear. DoD is looking to train people who will contribute to the defense effort of the United States. When filling out the application section that says "summarize the objectives of your educational program and your long-range professional goals," then, it only makes sense to remember the reason the fellowship was constructed in the first place and respond to that expectation.

Every application will directly or obliquely indicate why a fellowship has been constructed. Winners of awards will be those who, in addition to other qualities, have indicated that they intend, either during their graduate years or in their postgraduate careers, to fulfill an agency's purpose in constructing the fellowships in the first place.

4. **Some fellowships have paybacks.** If so, be sure that you understand the nature of the payback. The 1993–1994 Department of Defense Acquisition Scholarship Program clearly indicates the deal in the application: "each scholarship recipient must sign an agreement to

serve as a full-time civilian employee in an acquisition position in a DoD component . . . for a period of one calendar year for each year of school, or part of a school year, for which the student receives scholarship assistance." You need to decide whether you are willing to make the commitment required before you apply, or certainly before you accept this type of fellowship.

5. **Most of the fellowships in this category are highly competitive.** This is certainly true for the Hughes, Ford, Javits, Mellon, and NSF fellowships. Every single component in the application is important. *Grades must be great, GREs impressive, questions answered thoughtfully, and references glowing.* Many of these items are under your control. Certainly you can work and rework the application statements and have them reviewed by faculty or administrative mentors. Finding the most appropriate and enthusiastic references is crucial to success. Being very careful in dealing with these applications is important.

6. **Make sure everything you have written is easy to read.** Imagine sitting in a hotel room for three to five days reading application after application. This is what reviewers do. Therefore, you need to do whatever you can to make the application easy to read. If you are completing the application on a typewriter or printer, do not use a condensed, small typeface that is either too dark or too light. Be sure your ribbon is new and your printhead clean. Giving your reviewers eyestrain is a sure way to tax their patience and put the application in a bad light. If you fill out the basic information area by hand, be sure your writing is very legible. In a word, make certain everything you send is easy to read.

7. **If an award is denied and reapplication is an option, write the agency for reviewers' comments.** Most are willing to accommodate such requests; the few that do not usually say so in the application.

Specific Fellowship Opportunities

The following eleven fellowships include those that offer the largest number of awards as well as representative fellowships showing the range of student interests available. Most are government-funded. If the fellowship that interests you is not listed here, you should be able to find one or more with a similar focus and requirements. As usual, remember to check the application packet itself for up-to-date information.

All information, except the author's advice, is taken from the actual application packets, award announcements, and other documents written by administrative agencies, or on the basis of calls to the individual agencies. Every effort is made to use the same language as that on the application or to paraphrase or summarize that language. For ease of reading, quotation marks are used only to draw special attention to important application sections.

1. Department of Defense Acquisition Scholarships (MBA)[1]

Administrative Agency: U.S. Department of Defense.

Address: Defense Acquisition Scholarship Program
Northeast Consortium for Engineering Education
1101 Massachusetts Avenue
St. Cloud, FL 34769
Phone: 407-892-6146

Deadline: Mid-March.

Award Notification: Mid-May.

Number of Awards: 10–12 per competition.

Average Number of Applicants: 100 per competition.

Award Amount: $13,000 stipend for an academic year or $15,000 for a full year; a maximum of $14,500 for tuition; $500 for books, equipment, and supplies; and a $1,000 allowance paid to the student's department.

Application Form: The form should be available in the business school career center, library, or MBA program office. If not, the applicant should write to the funding agency two months before the deadline.

Purpose of Grant/Fellowship and Restrictions: Funding is targeted to students entering MBA programs in the fields of program management; communications/computer systems; contracting and purchasing; industrial property management; systems planning, research, development, and engineering test and evaluation engineering; manufacturing and production; quality assurance; acquisition logistics; and business, cost estimating, and financial audition. The objective of the program is to qualify personnel for civilian acquisition positions in the Department of Defense (DoD).

1. Based on the 1993–1994 Defense Acquisition Scholarships, U.S. Department of Defense.

Length of Award: One year with probable second year depending upon success in program and ability to complete degree in the second year.

Applicant Eligibility: The applicant should be a U.S. citizen and should possess high standardized test scores, strong letters of reference, and 3.00 out of 4.00 CGPA. The applicant must be willing to abide by payback agreement (see below); must have been accepted for enrollment or be currently enrolled as a full-time student in an MBA degree-granting program at an accredited institution, and must be in the process of completing or having completed an undergraduate degree in the physical sciences, mathematics, or a business-related discipline.

Application Requirements: Application form, including an Application for Federal Employment form; official transcripts; three letters of reference; GMAT or GRE scores; and official proof of acceptance at an accredited institution in an MBA program.

Conditions of the award require that an awardee must agree to remain enrolled in a field acceptable to the DoD and to accept, if offered within a reasonable time frame, a full-time acquisition position in the DoD and remain employed at the DoD for one calendar year for every year of graduate school support. Failure to fulfill the employment requirement mandates repayment of the scholarship. The DoD is not required to offer a position to an awardee; if a position is not offered, the awardee is under no obligation to repay the scholarship either by in-kind service or with currency.

Application Comments and Advice: The application is straightforward and uncomplicated.

Part 1 requests mostly demographic information.

Part 2 provides areas for (1) narrative explanations of honors, awards, scholarships, and leadership experiences relevant to the academic field and (2) a concise statement summarizing educational background and professional goals. (An extra sheet of paper is allowed and should be used, remembering, however, that brevity is encouraged.) Although it is not requested, a description of the course of study in the MBA program and how that will lead to the professional goals is recommended. Part 2 also requires (3) a description of experiences relating to the educational background described in (2) with emphasis on research experiences, volunteer activities, and work experience. Extra paper is allowed again, and you should take advantage of that opportunity. Items (2) and (3) should be seen as two parts of a whole and should be written to complement each other.

The payback requirement is more than reasonable. Working for the

Department of Defense is a good career or a good credential for moving on into the corporate world. Nonetheless, applicants should think through the obligaitons this award incurs before applying and absolutely before accepting a fellowship. A call to the DoD to determine what sorts of jobs are usually offered would be prudent.

2. Department of Defense Graduate Fellowships (Science/Mathematics/Engineering)[2]

Note that, unlike the Defense Acquisition Fellowship listed above, none of the fellowships in this category have a work-related payback requirement.

A. National Defense Science and Engineering Graduate Fellowships

Administrative Agency: Department of Defense.

Adress: NDSEG Fellowship Program
200 Park Drive, Suite 211, P.O. Box 13444
Research Triangle Park, NC 27709-3444
Phone: 919-549-8505

Deadline: Mid-January.

Award Notification: Mid-April.

Number of Awards: Approximately 90 per competition.

Average Number of Applicants: 2,700 per competition. (550 awards in four years with 10,800 applications).

Award Amount: $16,000 stipend in 1994–1995; $17,000 in 1995–1996. $18,000 stipend in 1996–1997. Full tuition and fees are paid to the awardee's institution and $2,000 is given to the awardee's department. Disabled awardees will be evaluated for increased funding to help with special expenses.

Application Form: The form should be available in science departments, the undergraduate college administrative office, the graduate school

2. Based on the 1994–1995 Department of Defense Graduate Fellowships, U.S. Department of Defense.

office, or the career center on campus, or directly from the address above.

Purpose of Grant/Fellowship and Restrictions: The object is to support students engaged in doctoral work at U.S. institutions in mathematics or physical, biological, ocean, and engineering sciences who are focusing on: aeronautical and astronautical engineering; biosciences (including toxicology); chemical engineering; cognitive, neural, and behavioral sciences; computer science; electrical engineering; geosciences; manufacturing sciences and engineering; materials science and engineering; mechanical engineering; naval architecture and ocean engineering; oceanography; physics. The DoD hopes to increase the number of people trained in areas of military importance. Awards do not incur any military or other service obligation.

Length of Award: Three years (12 months of support per year).

Applicant Eligibility: The applicant must be a U.S. citizen or a native resident of a possession of the United States (U.S. national) and have received a bachelor's degree prior to enrolling in the graduate program. Applicants should be at or near the beginning of their graduate study.

Application Requirements: Application Parts 1 and 2; official transcripts; and three letters of reference on DoD forms. GRE general test scores are highly recommended.

One application may be used to apply for any or all of the fellowships offered in this section (**2A**, **2B**, and **2C**) although the application must be copied if applying for two or more programs since a separate, complete application is required for each. All data for each application should be sent in one package if possible. A referee can, for example, put the letter of recommendation in an envelope with his or her signature across the seal and give it to the applicant for submission.

Applicants do not have to have been accepted into a program at the time of application but must have been accepted into a program in order to receive the award.

Application Comments and Advice: Since this application serves three fellowships, the instructions must be read very carefully to avoid confusion.

Part 1 requests basic demographic information such as name, address, minority status, and so on.

Part 2 (1) requests information about honors and activities. The preference here is for entries that are relevant to academic work. This is not the place for describing, for example, social fraternities. Think about which honors and activities would appeal most to the purpose of the fellowship and list them in that order. The agency is looking for proof of academic, especially scientific, ability and commitment, not a demonstration of a broad diversity of interests.

Part 2 (2) provides an opportunity to detail an educational plan and long-range professional goals. The more specific and detailed, the more believable the plan. Talking to a faculty member in the field is helpful with this part. Remember that the objective of the program is to support graduate work that is or will increase the pool of people who do research crucial to military defense. Reviewers are looking for academically well-grounded, enthusiastic, and committed people. An extra sheet of paper is permissible and should be used, since only a little over three inches are allocated on the form.

Part 2 (3) asks for a description (again extra paper is permissible) of experiences important to Part 2 (2). The agency is trying to determine what events relative to your academic, scientific background were in-strumental in inspiring the graduate and postgraduate plans described in Part 2 (2). This section gives evidence and substance to the plan. Think of it as the proof to a theorem. The two sections must make sense together. First describe the experiences that are most closely related to your field. Experiences that are somewhat less relevant should come next, and so on.

Reference Evaluations should be filled out by scientists and engi-neers who are most familiar with your academic potential—perhaps a faculty member or the leader of a lab in which you did research. Remember that referees are asked to comment on your potential as a scientist/engineer, your academic strengths and weaknesses, your un-dergraduate academic performance, and your technical judgment. All referees must be able to write enthusiastically to these issues.

B. Office of Naval Research Graduate Fellowships

Administrative Agency: American Society of Engineering Education.

Address: American Society of Engineering Education (ASEE)
        1818 N Street NW, Suite 600
        Washington, DC 20036
        Phone: 202-331-3525

Deadline: Late January.

Award Notification: Mid-April.

Number of Awards: As many as 50 per competition.

Average Number of Applicants: 1,000 per competition.

Award Amounts: Same as **1A**.

Application Form: Same as **1A**.

Purpose of Grant/Fellowship and Restrictions: The awards are intended to support doctoral study and research of importance to the U.S. Navy in: electrical engineering (integrated circuit design and fabrication, communications, solid state devices, electromagnetic, signal processing, quantum electronic); mathematics (applied mathematics, mathematical statistics, discrete mathematics, computational mathematics); physics (laser physics and quantum optics, surface physics, physical acoustics, underwater acoustics, opto-electronics, atomic and molecular physics, plasma physics); chemistry (polymer chemistry, solid state chemistry, surface chemistry, organic/organometallic chemistry, electrochemistry); computer science (systems, artificial intelligence, algorithms and software, architecture, robotics, manufacturing); materials science (processing science, composites and fibrous materials, corrosion and interfacial science, welding and adhesion, energetic materials synthesis, mechanical behavior of advanced materials); aerospace/mechanical engineering (fluid dynamics, computational mechanics, energy conversion, solid mechanics, manufacturing engineering, structural mechanics, structural acoustics, precision engineering); biological/biomedical sciences (biopolymers/biomaterials, molecular biology, cell biology, sensory systems); cognitive and neural sciences (computational neuroscience, neuroscience, bioengineering); and naval architecture and ocean engineering (ship structures, ship hydrodynamics, ocean engineering, remote sensing). Secretary of the navy fellowships are also available in oceanography (all fields of oceanography, marine meteorology, ocean acoustics and optics, geological acoustics and optics, geological/geophysical processes).

Length of Award: Same as **1A**.

Applicant Eligibility: The applicant must be a U.S. citizen who has not attended graduate school since receiving a bachelor's degree.

Application Requirements: Same as **1A**, except GRE general test scores required.

During the summer, fellows may continue research at a naval laboratory. A $2,000 additional stipend is available to cover travel, room, and board. A faculty advisor's visit to the lab will also be paid.

Application Comments and Advice: Same as **1A**.

C. United States Air Force Laboratory Graduate Fellowships

Administrative Agency: U.S. Air Force.

Address: SCEEE-Fellowship Program
1101 Massachusetts Avenue
St. Cloud, FL 34769-3733
Phone: 407-892-6146

Deadline: Late January.

Award Notification: Mid-April.

Number of Awards: 25 per competition.

Average Number of Applicants: 1,200–1,500 per competition.

Award Amount: Same as **1A**.

Application Form: Same as **1A**.

Purpose of Grant/Fellowship and Restrictions: The Air Force is interested in educating people in areas critical to its operation: aeronautical and astronautical engineering; behavioral sciences; biomedical engineering; chemistry and chemical engineering; computer science and computer modeling; electrical engineering; geophysics and meteorology; industrial and civil engineering; life sciences, biology and biophysics; materials science, ceramic engineering, and metallurgy; mathematics; mechanical engineering; physics.

Length of Award: Same as **1A**.

Applicant Eligibility: Applicants must be U.S. citizens who have received their bachelor's degree before or during the application year.

Preference is given to undergraduates and first-year graduate students.

Application Requirements: Same as **1A**, except that the applicant must indicate three laboratory affiliation choices.

Awardees are required to affiliate with an Air Force laboratory that they will visit, be assigned a mentor, and spend one summer doing research, for which they will receive extra financial support. Laboratory preferences can be based on disciplinary interests. The application provides laboratory research interest information.

Application Comments and Advice: Same as **1A**.

3. Ford Foundation Predoctoral Fellowships for Minorities[3]

Administrative Agency: National Research Council.

Address: National Research Council
The Fellowship Office
2101 Constitutional Avenue
Washington, DC 20418
Phone: 202-334-2872

Deadline: Early November for Part 1, early December for Part 2, references by late January.

Award Notification: Early April.

Number of Awards: 55 per competition.

Average Number of Applicants: 1,000 per competition.

Award Amount: $11,500 stipend for nine- or twelve-month tenures, depending upon the discipline, for three years; $6,000 to the institution for tuition and fees; $1,000 to the department to enhance the minority recruiting program. Stipends must be used within five years. (Years need not be consecutive so that fellows may serve as teaching assistants or participate in other departmental activities.)

3. Based on the 1993–1994 Ford Foundation Predoctoral Fellowships for Minorities, National Research Council.

Application Form: The form should be available in the undergraduate college administrative office, the graduate school office, or the career center on campus, or directly from the address above.

Purpose of Grant/Fellowship and Restrictions: The objective is to increase the pool of minority students with PhD and ScD degrees who will become college and university professors. Students are supported in doctoral programs at any accredited U.S. institution in the fields of behavioral and social sciences, humanities, engineering, mathematics, physical sciences, biological sciences, and interdisciplinary programs involving the above disciplines. Support is *not available* to students in business administration and management, health sciences, public health, home economics, library science, speech pathology and audiology, personnel and guidance, social work, fine arts, performing arts, education, any work leading to a terminal master's degree, doctorates in education or fine arts, or professional degrees including business, law, or medicine.

Length of Award: Three years.

Applicant Eligibility: Applicants must be U.S. citizens or native residents of a possession of the U.S. (U.S. nationals); Alaskan Natives, Native American Indians, Black/African Americans, Mexican Americans/Chicanos, Native Pacific Islanders (Polynesian or Micronesian), or Puerto Ricans; and college seniors. Graduate student applicants may have earned no more than 30 semester hours (45 quarter hours) of graduate-level credit in the fields listed above. Anyone holding a doctoral degree in any field is not eligible.

Application Requirements: GRE scores from test taken no later than December of the application year; official transcripts; two letters of reference; all parts of the application. The application is also used for the dissertation fellowship competition, so read the directions carefully and do not respond to "dissertation applicant only" sections.

Application Comments and Advice: Be sure to understand the various sections of the application. A sheet entitled "Outline for Preparing a Clear, Concise Predoctoral Application" should be read carefully and followed scrupulously.

The "Proposed Plan of Graduate Study" section gives you the opportunity to describe in narrative form what exactly you expect to accomplish and pursue in graduate school or how your educational objectives will be accomplished through a graduate program. In addition, you need to describe the institution at which you propose to study. The reviewers will be interested to see how your particular institution can be related to your proposed plan. That means describing how specific professors or specific courses at your institution which will facilitate your plan.

An opportunity to describe "Previous Research Experience" is also available and is an important component.

Part 2 contains two sections that are especially important. One section asks for a short summary of professional goals. The other asks for a description of other kinds of experiences (volunteer work, leadership activities, etc.) that are meaningful to your career goals and proposed course of study. There is no limit on how much you should write; one to three pages is suggested. All the information gathered from the sections described above will be read as parts of a whole, and so they should all hang together even though they are in separate areas.

To enhance the last section, you may include a resume (sometimes called a *curriculum vitae* in the academic world). The resume should include only information that is relevant to the pursuit of your intellectual interests, your graduate degree, and your career goals. All information should contribute to the reviewer's better understanding of your qualifications to pursue graduate work.

4. GEM Fellowship Program[4]

Administrative Agency: National Consortium for Graduate Degrees for Minorities in Engineering and Science, Inc. (GEM).

Address: GEM Fellowship Programs
P.O. Box 537
Notre Dame, IN 46556
Phone: 219-287-1097

Deadline: Early December.

Award Notification: Early February.

Number of Awards: 220 per competition in the master's in engineering; 30 in the PhD in science; 30 in the PhD in engineering.

Average Number of Applicants: 1,000 per competition in the master's in engineering; 100 in the PhD in science; 100 in the PhD in engineering.

4. Based on the 1993–1994 GEM Fellowships, National GEM Center.

Award Amount: $6,000 stipend per year for the master's degree and $12,000 per year for the doctoral degree. Tuition and fees are covered; amount depends on the institution.

Application Form: The form should be available in the undergraduate or graduate administrative office, career center, or minority advertisement office or from the above address.

Purpose of Grant/Fellowship and Restrictions: The purpose of the award is to increase the presence of minority students in graduate programs in science and engineering. Awardees may pursue an M.S. degree in engineering, a doctoral degree in engineering, or a doctoral degree in the natural sciences (biology, chemistry, earth and planetary sciences, mathematics, or physics).

Length of Award: Two years for master's students; five years for doctoral students. (GEM supports the first year of doctoral study and the home institution funds the last four years.)

Applicant Eligibility: The applicant must be a U.S. citizen of American Indian, Black American, Mexican American, or Puerto Rican ethnicity with a minimum GPA of 3.00 out of 4.00. Those pursuing the master's in engineering must have an undergraduate major in the same graduate discipline; those seeking a doctoral in science may have an undergraduate major in any natural science; those seeking a doctorate in engineering may have an undergraduate major in any engineering discipline.

Application Requirements: Application form; transcripts; application to three GEM-affiliated schools for applicants not yet enrolled in a graduate program; three letters of recommendation. Doctoral applicants may submit a one-page Statement of Purpose.

Awards may only be used at the 70 designated GEM member universities.

Application Comments and Advice: The application is relatively modest in its requirements. Only doctoral students may submit a one-page written narrative. That statement should include a description of study and research interests and a proposed course of study as related to career goals. Master's students are given one paragraph in which to explain their expectations and study objectives, interests, and career goals. A supplementary section should be used to add to either the one-paragraph statement or to enhance honors, awards, and other activities relevant to your chosen field of study.

5. Howard Hughes Predoctoral Fellowships in the Biological Sciences[5]

Administrative Agency: National Research Council.

Address: Hughes Predoctoral Fellowships
Fellowship Office
National Research Council
2101 Constitution Avenue
Washington, DC 20418
Phone: 202-334-2872

Deadline: Early November for Part 1; early December for Part 2.

Award Notification: Early April.

Number of Awards: 66 per competition.

Average Number of Applicants: 1,500 per competition.

Award Amount: $14,000 stipend for 1994–1995; $11,000 for tuition; $1,700 paid to the institution to cover some of the fellow's costs in the areas of health insurance, books, supplies, computer expenses, travel to scientific meetings, summer tuition, and secretarial/clerical services related to program costs.

Application Form: The application should be available from the biology department, undergraduate or graduate administrative office, financial aid office, or career center or from the address above.

Purpose of Grant/Fellowship and Restrictions: The award is intended to increase the pool of qualified students pursuing doctoral degrees in research in the biomedical sciences.

Length of Award: Three consecutive years, with a possible additional two years.

5. Based on the 1994–1995 Howard Hughes Predoctoral Fellowships in Biological Sciences, National Research Council.

Applicant Eligibility: The awards are open to foreign nationals and U.S. citizens who are at or near the beginning of their PhD or ScD work in biochemistry, biophysics, biostatistics, cell biology and regulation, developmental biology, epidemiology, genetics, immunology, mathematical biology, microbiology, neuroscience, pharmacology, physiology, structural biology, or virology.

Application Requirements: Parts 1 and 2 of the application; GRE scores (subject test is desirable); TOEFL scores for foreign nationals whose first language is not English; official transcripts; GPA report form; and four reference reports.

Application Comments and Advice: Part 1 is straightforward and relatively simple. Part 2 includes a two-page instruction sheet that should be read very closely.

Four sections of Part 2 are the most important. The "Proposed Plan of Study or Research" is a two-page opportunity to describe specific research interests, questions, or problems to be pursued in graduate school. The object of the statement is to show how motivated, enthusiastic, independent, creative, forward-thinking, thoughtful, and well informed you are in your chosen field. For those who have done an honors thesis or special rotation this is a great opportunity to describe that experience relative to specific plans for study and research in graduate school.

A second important section allows you to describe in two pages "Previous Research Experience." Here you should provide evidence that you are familiar with and capable of doing the types of research that will be expected in graduate school and that you have written about in your "Proposed Plan for Study and Research." If you are doing genetics and have spent the summer working as a lab assistant doing DNA experiments, describe that experience in this section. If your previous research provided the inspiration for your "Proposed Plan of Study and Research," so much the better. Work relevant to the field done beyond the bachelor's degree should also be described, and you should include a list of any publications and presentations.

A third section asks for a description of experiences that have inspired or are relevant to the "Proposed Plan." These could include leadership roles in honor societies or volunteer or work experiences related to the field. Do not repeat what you already said in the "Previous Research Experience" section.

The fourth section in this part of the application really asks you to summarize the educational plans described in the "Proposed Plan of Study or Research" relevant to your career goals.

The four sections should be seen as parts of a whole. Candidates should be careful not to be repetitive and should use each area to present new information that ties directly to the other sections.

6. Indian Education Fellowship Program[6]

Administrative Agency: U.S. Department of Education.

Address: Branch Chief
Office of Indian Education
Department of Education
400 Maryland Avenue SW
Washington, DC 20202
Phone: 202-260-3774

Deadline: Late January.

Award Notification: No published date for notification.

Number of Awards: 53 new awards per competition; 73 continuing.

Average Number of Applicants: 570 per competition in 1992.

Award Amount: Average stipend of $12,590.

Application Form: Applicants should check the undergraduate or graduate administrative office or write to the above address.

Purpose of Grant/Fellowship and Restrictions: The purpose of the award is to support Native American students doing graduate-level work in medicine, psychology, law, education, or related fields. Support is also available to students pursuing undergraduate work in business administration, engineering, natural resources, or related fields.

Length of Award: One year with renewals possible.

Applicant Eligibility: An applicant must be a U.S. citizen who holds membership in a tribe, band, or groups terminated since 1940 and those recognized by the state in which they reside, or be a descendant in the first or second degree of any individual described above, or be

6. Based on the 1993–1994 Indian Fellowships, U.S. Department of Education.

considered by the Secretary of the Interior to be an Indian for any purpose, or be an Eskimo, Aleut, or other Alaskan Native. The applicant must be a full-time degree candidate at an accredited institution of higher education. Those holding a terminal degree in one of the fields given under Purpose of Grant/Fellowship and Restrictions, above, are not eligible to apply.

Application Requirements: Documentation of Indian ethnicity; official transcripts; standardized test scores; three letters of reference; and a written essay.

Application Comments and Advice: The most important application criterion is the academic record, to which 80 of the possible 100 points are allocated. Your academic record is determined by a review of your standardized test scores, official transcripts, and grade reports.

Ten points are allocated to leadership, which is judged through your documentation of your leadership positions and through references.

The final 10 points are allocated to the essay segment, in which you should assess your abilities in the areas of clear writing, commitment to your chosen field of study, and evidence that your chosen graduate program will facilitate your career, especially as a leader in the Indian community.

7. Jacob K. Javits Fellowships for the Arts, Humanities, and Social Sciences[7]

Administrative Agency: U.S. Department of Education.

Address: Jacob K. Javits Fellowship Program
P.O. Box 84
Washington, DC 20044
Phone: 800-4-FED-AID; 202-708-9415

Deadline: Late November. (The deadline has historically been very erratic for this fellowship; if applications are not available by October, the competition has probably been delayed, but will very likely be held.)

Award Notification: Mid-March.

7. Based on the 1994–1995 Jacob K. Javits Fellowships, U.S. Department of Education.

Number of Awards: 80–150 per competition, depending on congressional funding in any given year.

Average Number of Applicants: 3,000 per competition.

Award Amount: $14,000 stipend; $9,000 paid to the institution for tuition and fees.

Application Form: The application may be obtained from the undergraduate college or graduate school office or the career center on campus or directly from the address above.

Purpose of Grant/Fellowship and Restrictions: The award is intended to encourage and assist students in pursuing doctoral degrees in the humanities and social sciences and doctoral or master's of fine arts degrees in the arts. Nearly 100 subfields are defined in the application. The award does *not* fund doctoral programs in divinity, engineering, natural sciences, medicine, social work, clinical psychology, and education.

Length of Award: Up to four years.

Applicant Eligibility: Applicants may be U.S. citizens, U.S. nationals, permanent residents of U.S., or permanent residents of the Trust Territory of the Pacific Islands.

Application Requirements: GRE general test scores for those applying in the humanities and social sciences; transcripts; three letters of recommendation on official forms; all application parts. Those applying in the arts should also provide audio tapes, slides, photographs, video tapes, manuscripts, or other supporting materials as applicable.

Applicants in the arts should pay particular attention to the restrictions put on supporting materials. For example, audio cassette tapes only may be sent, and these may contain no more than 5 minutes of recording; no more than 20 slides are allowable; and so on.

Application Comments and Advice: Javits is one application that actually includes a section explaining how points are allocated in making award decisions. This gives the potential applicant a sense of whether applying makes sense. Out of 400 possible points, 150 are allocated to academic record, which means grade point average, quality and relevance of previous courses of study, and GRE scores. Given the number of applicants, if your GREs are not in the ninetieth percentile or higher and your GPA is less than 3.5 out of 4, your chances of getting enough points in this category are slim.

An additional 100 points are reserved for references testifying to your breadth of academic knowledge, intellectual curiosity, written and oral communication skills, research skills, motivation, perseverance, creativity, and originality. References must be unfailingly enthusiastic to be effective.

Another 100 points are assigned to your personal statement. Two pages are allotted to the applicant for a description of how your proposed plan of study and intellectual interest will facilitate your career goals. The plan should be very focused on the particular field you are pursuing. You should demonstrate a superior wealth of information about the field (both in the arts and sciences and in the arts fields), a well-developed intellectual curiosity, a willingness to persist to an advanced degree, a commitment to the field, originality, and creativity (especially in the arts). The reviewers are looking for well-focused individuals who are intellectually and creatively enthusiastic and motivated.

Since career goals are a sign that you have thoroughly investigated your employment path, you should develop this section thoroughly; it should work well with your plan of studies and intellectual interest. This is especially important if you have not yet started a graduate program.

In the past the Javits program supported graduate students at all levels. In the spring of 1994 the Javits Board decided that the program will limit application from enrolled graduate students to those who have no more than 30 semester hours of graduate credit at the time of application.

The last 50 points are reserved for honors and awards. Twelve lines are allowed on the application. Briefly list your honors, awards, presentations, and publications on these lines, and then, if it makes sense, supplement that list with an extra sheet. This is an area that can make or break an application, and it should be taken seriously. Applicants should be sure to note bachelor or master's theses in this section, as well as all graduation honors.

8. Mellon Fellowships in Humanistic Studies[8]

The guidelines for this competition have change substantially in the

---

8. Based on the 1993–1994 Andrew W. Mellon Fellowships in Humanistic Studies, Woodrow Wilson National Fellowship Foundation.

last several years; so a current program brochure is an absolute necessity.

Administrative Agency: The Woodrow Wilson National Fellowship Foundation.

Address: Andrew W. Mellon Fellowships in Humanistic Studies
The Woodrow Wilson Foundation
CN 5329
Princeton, NJ 08542-0288
Phone: 609-452-7007

Deadline: Early December. An application must be requested in early November.

Award Notification: Late January to early February for semi-finalist notification; early April for awards.

Number of Awards: 80 per competition for 1994–1995.

Average Number of Applicants: 1,107 per competition. 209 were selected as finalists and 81 awards were granted in 1993.

Award Amount: $12,750 stipend; tuition and standard fees depending upon the institution. Fellows may not accept supplemental, institutional awards nor may they function as teaching assistants.

Application Form: Many campuses have a faculty member who functions as a Mellon advisor and has informational brochures available. Persons wishing to receive an application must write to the address above requesting an application and must submit with that request the following: full name; current mailing address; mailing address January–March (during the interview period); undergraduate institution and major; year of graduation; and intended discipline in graduate school.

Purpose of Grant/Fellowship and Restrictions: The programmatic purpose is to encourage exceptional students to enroll in PhD programs in the United States and Canada. The basic intent is to facilitate the development of scholars and faculty in American studies, art history, classics, comparative literature, cultural anthropology, English literature, foreign languages and literatures, history, history and philosophy of science, political philosophy, musicology, philosophy, and religion.

Length of Award: One year.

Applicant Eligibility: Applicants should be college seniors or recent graduates (within 5 years) who are U.S. citizens or permanent residents and have not begun any graduate program.

Application Requirements: Application form; GRE test scores; official transcripts; three letters of recommendation; foreign language competence form; and 1,000-word or less statement of intellectual interests.

Applicants who have previously applied and been rejected may not reapply.

Application Comments and Advice: Applicants who successfully pass through the first assessment level are invited to be interviewed in their region. From this group, approximately 40 percent were funded in 1993. While high GREs and GPAs are not the only criteria, they are important. The foundation is concerned about your references' opinions of your promise as an academic scholar and faculty member; so be sure references address these areas very specifically.

The essay (1,000 words or less) requires a delineation of "intellectual interests," which should be read as interests specific to your departmental or field choice. If you intend to pursue a concentration in religions of classical antiquity, for example, those are the intellectual interests that you should substantively describe. What events (reading a certain book, hearing a specific lecture, attending a particular class) first interested you in your field? What subsequent events helped form your knowledge base (a major in the field, a year of study abroad, a particular research project, an archaeological excavation, etc.)? The background should lay the groundwork for a particular plan for graduate study, which might involve taking certain kinds of courses, study abroad, and specific research interests. This description should then lead to a discussion of your career goals in academia. The Foundation wants to support students who are well grounded from undergraduate college in their field, who demonstrate a commitment to academic research, and who they feel will complete a doctoral thesis and become a member of the academic community after graduation.

The information in the essay is usually the same as that requested on the typical graduate application. Many candidates, in both cases, commonly revert back to an undergraduate application mode by trying to look diverse in interests and widespread in activities, or clever. Don't do it. This sort of application is for the serious scholar. Cut to the chase with a very focused description of your field and specific intellectual background, detailed graduate plans, and career goals. Descriptions of a wide range of activities will worry readers, who are looking for future academics who are willing to immerse themselves exclusively in graduate work for six to eight years.

At the end of the "statement of intellectual interest" section, a request is made for academic honors, senior level courses, and projects. Projects described should be relevant to your intellectual interests. A description of your senior or honors thesis would be of more interest than delineation of your involvement in a student government project, unless that project relates directly to your intellectual interests.

9. National Hispanic Scholarships[9]

Administrative Agency: National Hispanic Scholarship Fund.

Address: National Hispanic Scholarship Fund
P.O. Box 728
Novato, CA 94948
Phone: 415-892-9971

Deadline: April 1–June 15.

Award Notification: After February 1 of following year.

Number of Awards: Around 3,000 per competition.

Average Number of Applicants: 10,000 per competition.

Award Amount: $500–$1,000 stipend.

Application Form: The form may be obtained from the college or graduate administrative office or multicultural affairs office, or by writing to the address above.

Purpose of Grant/Fellowship and Restrictions: The purpose of the award is to provide support to Hispanic American students in higher education in associate, bachelor's, master's, and doctoral degree programs of any type. Students must demonstrate financial need.

Length of Award: One year.

9. Based on the 1994–1995 National Hispanic Scholarships, National Hispanic Scholarship Fund.

Applicant Eligibility: Applicants must be U.S. citizens or U.S. permanent residents of Hispanic parentage who can demonstrate financial need. Students must be enrolled full time in any graduate degree program; students in non-traditional, weekend, night, or part-time programs are not eligible to apply, nor are fully employed persons.

Application Requirements: Application form; transcripts; letter of recommendation; personal statement; and eventual verification of enrollment and attendance.

For the purposes of the application, Hispanic parentage includes Mexican American, Central American, Caribbean (Hispanic), Cuban, Puerto Rican, and South American.

Application Comments and Advice: Equitable geographic distribution of fellowships figures into the awards process. One of the most important components is a two-page personal statement that requests a delineation of family background, a description of financial need, current educational status, career goals, and "how you plan to help NHSF in helping others like yourself in the future," which can be read as a future commitment to help others when you have made it through school and are successful. The application allows additional comments, which should include honors and awards and a description of your current and planned course of study. Candidates are encouraged to conceive of this exercise as a form of interview with the selection committee. The committee is clearly looking for motivated students with financial need who are committed to completing their education and who, in the future, are dedicated to helping others of Hispanic parentage realize their goals.

10. National Science Foundation Graduate Research Fellowships in the Sciences, Social Sciences, and Engineering and National Science Foundation Minority Fellowships and Women in Engineering Awards[10]

Administrating Agency: Oak Ridge Associated Universities.

Address: NSF Graduate Research Fellowship Program
Oak Ridge Associated Universities

10. Based on the 1994–1995 National Science Foundation Graduate Research Fellowships, Oak Ridge Associated Universities.

P.O. Box 3010
Oak Ridge, TN 37831-3010
Phone: 615-483-3344

Deadline: Early November for Part 1; early December for Part 2.

Award Notification: Early spring.

Number of Awards: 1,000 per competition.

Average Number of Applicants: 8,600 per competition.

Award Amount: $14,000 stipend; $7,500 toward tuition, plus a $1,000 one-time international research allowance for students who need to conduct research abroad.

Application Form: The application may be obtained from science and social science departments, graduate or undergraduate administrative offices, or campus research office, or by writing to the above address.

Purpose of Grant/Fellowship and Restrictions: The award is intended to increase the number of people receiving master's or doctoral degrees in mathematics; physical, biological, engineering, behavioral, and social sciences; history of science; and philosophy of science. Support is *not* available for training in clinical programs, business, management, history, social work, medicine, law, dentistry, or public health programs. Minorities and women underrepresented in their chosen field of study are especially encouraged to apply.

Length of Award: Three years.

Applicant Eligibility: Applicants are those in their senior year of college or in their first year of graduate school who have taken no more than 20 semester or 30 quarter hours of graduate credit. Minority members and women in engineering candidates who have no more than 30 hours or 45 semester hours of graduate credit are eligible. Applicants must be U.S. citizens, U.S. nationals, or U.S. permanent residents.

Application Requirements: Part 1 requests demographic and educational background information. Completion of this short form triggers the mailing to the applicant of Part 2. Also required are official transcripts, an undergraduate GPA form, a course report form, GRE scores, four references, a proposed plan of study or research, and a form detailing previous research experience.

Application Comments and Advice: Part 1 is straightfoward and simple. Part 2 includes a colorful two-page instruction sheet, which should be read very closely.

Four sections of Part 2 are the most important. The "Proposed Plan of Study or Research" is a two-page opportunity to describe specific research interests, questions, and plans to be pursued in graduate school. If you do not yet have a research plan, then you should define the sorts of academic interests you have and how those interests will facilitate your career plans. The object of the statement is to show how motivated, enthusiastic, independent, creative, thoughtful, and well informed you are about your chosen field. A vague interest in science is not as persuasive as a description of specific research interests and how your graduate program will facilitate those interests.

A second important section allows you to describe in two pages your "Previous Research Experience." This can be viewed as evidence that you are familiar with and capable of doing the types of research that will be expected in graduate school and that you have written about in the "Proposed Plan for Study and Research" section. If you have done an honors thesis or project, this is a great opportunity to describe that experience. A person going into anthropology might have spent the summer doing ethnography in Kenya. That would be a great experience for this section. If the previous research is inspiration for the "Proposed Plan of Study and Research" so much the better.

A third section asks for a description of the experiences that inspired or are relevant to your "Proposed Plan." These could include leadership roles in honor societies or volunteer or work experiences related to the field. If you are interested in political science, volunteer work with a political campaign or work with student government would fit nicely into this area. The object is to not repeat what is written in the "Previous Research Experience" area. An extra sheet of paper is allowed in this section. One should view this section as supplemental to "Previous Research Experience."

The fourth section in this part of the application really asks the candidate to summarize the "Proposed Plan of Study or Research" relevant to career goals.

The four sections should be viewed as parts of a whole. Candidates should be careful not to be repetitive and should use each area for new information which ties directly to the other sections.

11. National Security Education Fellowships for Non-Western Foreign Language and Area Studies[11]

Administrative Agency: Academy for Educational Development.

Address: Academy for Educational Development
1875 Connecticut Avenue NW, 9th Floor
Washington, DC 20009
Phone: 800-498-9360 (for application)
202-884-8285

Deadline: Early March.

Award Notification: To be announced.

Number of Awards: 200–250 per competition.

Award Amount: $8,000–$25,000 stipend; tuition and fees for graduate studies that have to do with foreign language and area studies.

Application Form: Application must be made through a college or university. Students should see the program officer on campus. Special arrangements can be made for those who are not on campus; non-student applicants should call the agency for more information. As this book goes to press, the application is being revised and requirements may vary from what is presented here.

Purpose of Grant/Fellowship and Restrictions: The program had its first competition in the spring of 1994. The aim of the award is to educate U.S. citizens in non-western cultures in the hope of strengthening U.S. economic competitiveness and of enhancing international cooperation and security. It intentionally supports language and area studies other than those targeted by traditional study abroad programs. In general this fellowship does *not* support study or research related to or in Western Europe, Canada or Scandinavia.

The program will support anywhere from a summer semester to three years of study and research. Doctoral students may apply for up

11. Based on the 1994–1995 National Security Education Program Graduate Program in Professional and Other Disciplines with an International Component, Academy for Educational Development.

to three years of support. Students in professional programs such as law, business, social work, etc. may apply for up to two years of support. Applications that include a study abroad component are viewed as stronger than those that do not.

There is also a separate program for undergraduates from freshman through senior levels. This program offers 800 fellowships. Interested students should call the agency or see their campus advisor for more information.

Length of Award: One summer to three academic years.

Applicant Eligibility: Applicants should be U.S. citizens who have been accepted into or are enrolled in an accredited graduate degree program and are willing to enter a service agreement if awarded a fellowship. (See Special Application Information below.)

Application Requirements: Completed application; three letters of recommendation; language evaluation; budget; and on-campus committee evaluation.

There is a postfellowship service requirement. The objective is to require awardees to work in either education or government after graduation for a length of time to be specified upon awarding of the fellowship. Awardees should carefully consider this requirement before accepting a fellowship. If the awardee does not fulfill this contracted obligation, the fellowship becomes a student loan and is repayable to the government.

Application Comments and Advice: The application requires that you delineate a graduate plan, including a foreign language or area studies component. If you are a law student who is also getting a master's degree in Asian studies, for example, you want to describe your specific graduate school plans. Plans should include language and cultural study courses as well as career goals.

The program is interested in supporting study and research abroad. While it is possible to ask for support for study in the United States only, that does not appear prudent. It is also important to remember that the purpose of the program is to enhance United States economic competitive edge, U.S. cooperation with foreign cultures, and U.S. national security. One or all of these points should be addressed in application.

Since the program is new, it is hard to predict what type of application will be the most appealing to reviewers. Read the directions carefully and follow them scrupulously.

Further Reading. See Chapter 2.

Chapter 4
Study/Research Abroad

This chapter presents general information and application writing advice for the study/research abroad fellowships for which a person may apply. It also describes in detail certain specific fellowship opportunities, namely:

1. British Marshall Scholarships for Study in Great Britain
2. CSC-PRC Graduate Study/Dissertation Research in China
3. Deutscher Akademischer AustauschDienst Grants for Study and Research in Germany
4. Fulbright (IIE) Grants for Study, Research, and Teaching Abroad
5. Fulbright-Hays (DOE) Dissertation Research in Area Studies in Non-Western Countries
6. International Research and Exchange (IREX) Grants for Central and Eastern Europe, the former Soviet Union, and Mongolia
7. Japanese Government (Monbusho) Scholarships for Research Students
8. Rhodes Scholarships to Oxford University in Great Britain
9. Rotary Foundation Academic-Year Ambassadorial Scholarships
10. Social Science Research Council Fellowships

Fellowships in this section are of interest to: Junior and senior undergraduates; first- through fifth-year graduate students.

Fields funded by one or more of these fellowships: All academic and professional fields.

Degree programs funded by these fellowships: Master's and doctoral.

General Information

Undergraduate students are often interested in pursuing study/research programs in the year following graduation. Students in this category should start looking at Fulbright, Rotary, Rhodes, or Marshall programs during the spring semester of their junior year. This is especially true for the Rotary and Fulbright Fellowships. Almost all colleges and universities have information on these programs readily accessible to interested students. The potential for getting funded in this category is good for students who have sufficient language skills and interesting study plans or research projects and who have made connections abroad. While truly exceptional academic credentials are required for the Rhodes and Marshall, this is not necessarily the case for Rotary or Fulbright, where good language skills and good proposals for study or research are more important.

Students in many areas of graduate study may also be interested in study/research abroad, and opportunities are abundant. Anyone with the qualifications to go to school or conduct research in a foreign country should actively pursue fellowship and grant opportunities because the chances of getting partial or full financial support are very good.

General Application Advice

1. **Start early.** There are several reasons for starting early. The first is that many competitions, like the Fulbright, have a two-stage process in which applications are reviewed first in the United States and then in the host foreign country. Some competitions, like the Rotary, have a long process of review within the United States, where applications are considered at the local organizational level and then go on to regional and then national reviews. Some, including the Rhodes and Marshall, have an interviewing process for finalists.

Contacts abroad are often crucial to a successful application. These can be hard to come by, especially in less developed countries, where telephone and mail communications are problematic. Graduate students doing research should be especially careful to establish contacts sufficiently ahead of application deadlines. Funding agencies are wary of giving money to a student who has no connections with people abroad who will facilitate research. If, for example, access to archives is important for your research, then a letter from the archive should accompany the application assuring entry. If you intend to study a certain group of people, then be sure to include a letter from an expert in the field in the country assuring that such a thing is possible. Collaboration with researchers abroad must be verified, preferably in writing.

If you wish to study at a foreign institution, you should already be in contact with the program or, even better, have been admitted to the institution. All arrangements to do study/research abroad take more time than you imagine. Starting 18 months before the desired date of departure should be sufficient.

2. **Know a lot about the country you wish to study or carry out research.** A surprising number of applicants know something about the country within their field but hardly anything about the society in general. Since you must live successfully within the culture, you should demonstrate that you possess prior knowledge about the historical, political, and cultural milieu. This is especially important if the fellowship you seek has an interviewing process, like that of the Fulbright, Marshall, Monbusho, or Rhodes.

3. **Be relevant and country-specific about what you want to do.** It is not good enough, for example, just to want to study history in England. Study/research abroad funding agencies must be convinced that you have a compelling reason to go to the country to which you are applying. If you can get the information in the United States, why should the government or agency pay you to get it abroad? What is it that you can do in a foreign country that you cannot do at home? Researching the impact of the Romans on early English culture by analyzing the archaeological stratigraphy at sites located only in certain parts of England is much more compelling than simply studying Roman archaeology.

4. **Know the topic thoroughly.** Nothing makes a review panel happier than to see that you know the topic thoroughly. Just as the unexamined life to Socrates was not worth living, so the unexamined topic to a funding agency is not worth supporting. For graduate students, this means demonstrating an intimate understanding of what others in the field think about the topic through a review of the literature as well as detailing an acceptable methodology for approaching the research.

5. **Provide a reasonable timetable for accomplishing your study or research.** Creating a timetable is not easy. If you have no prior experience abroad, especially in research, it is hard to know what sounds feasible. Most applicants overstate the potential outcomes and therefore sound unreasonable. Talk to someone in the field who has done related research and find out what is doable within the proposed time constraints.

6. **Have language ability sufficient to carry out your study/research program and to live successfully within the culture.** Let's say

you want to study early Greek texts in Athens. You would need to demonstrate superior facility in classical Greek as well as a capability to negotiate the culture in modern Greek. A funding agency may be flexible where language training is difficult to obtain, but you must offer a convincing plan for acquiring the necessary language skill in the application. Many applications fail because, although the project was carefully researched, knowledge of the topic was extraordinary, the timeframe was reasonable, and faculty support was exceptionally strong, the review panel was just not convinced that the applicants' language skills were up to speed.

7. **Be sure your references are 100 percent behind the proposal.** Your references' enthusiasm for the project and the impression you will make abroad is very important. Since conditions in other countries often add impediments to successful completion of programs and projects, funding agencies are even more concerned than usual with the opinion of references. Be sure your references are appropriate to your application. Every doctoral student must have strong, unwavering support from her or his research director. Every undergraduate and graduate student needs at least three references who will assure review panels that the applicant is academically prepared to study or do research in another country, that adaptation to the new culture will be easy, and that the applicant will make a good impression as an American in the host country.

Specific Fellowship Opportunities

All information, except the author's advice, is taken from the actual application packets, award announcements, and other documents written by administrative agencies, or on the basis of calls to the individual agencies. Every effort is made to use the same language as that on the application or to paraphrase or summarize that language. For ease of reading, quotation marks are used only to draw special attention to important application sections.

1. British Marshall Scholarships for Study in Great Britain[1]

Administrative Agency: Marshall Aid Commemoration Commission.

Address: British Embassy
Cultural Department

1. Based on the 1993 British Marshall Scholarships, Marshall Aid Commemoration Commission.

3100 Massachusetts Avenue NW
Washington, DC 20008
Phone: 202-462-1340

Or contact the British Consulate-General in Chicago, Boston, San Francisco, or Atlanta.

Deadline: Mid-October.

Award Notification: Late November.

Number of Awards: Up to 40 per competition.

Average Number of Applicants: 800 per competition.

Award Amount: Stipend of £12,500, covering tuition, books, fees, travel, room, and board. A marriage allowance is possible for the second year only.

Application Form: Forms should be available through the undergraduate administrative offices on campus or by contacting the British Embassy in Washington or the Consulates-General listed under Address, above.

Purpose of Grant/Fellowship and Restrictions: The British Marshall Scholarships were created as an expression of appreciation for the Marshall Plan, which was developed following World War II to strengthen ties with the United States, and to improve the image of Great Britain among Americans. Each scholarship supports a student for two years of study leading to either a second undergraduate degree or a graduate degree at one of the 44 universities in Britain (England, Northern Ireland, Scotland, and Wales).

Length of Award: Two years, with possible third year, depending upon the academic program.

Applicant Eligibility: An applicant must be a U.S. citizen not older than 25 years of age, must have a GPA from sophomore through senior year of 3.7 or higher or an A− average or higher, and must have completed an undergraduate degree prior to the scholarship period. Applicants may not hold a British degree.

Application Requirements: Completed application form; two letters of reference; photograph; letter of endorsement from dean or employer;

transcripts; and narrative describing proposed course of study at specific universities.

Applicants are encouraged to consider study at British universities other than Oxford or Cambridge, although a high percentage of awards are made for study at these two institutions. Applicants interested in study in the fields of business and applied studies are especially desirable. Applicants in the fields of archaeology, anthropology, and earth and planetary sciences whose training may take them out of Britain during the scholarship period are not encouraged to apply. All qualifications being equal, preference will be given to unmarried students.

Application Comments and Advice: Because British universities differ significantly in organization and course structure from those in the United States, it is important to start gathering information about institutions and programs in the winter or early spring before the October deadline. Applicants who have not already taken a graduate degree or have not done some significant graduate work in the United States are not likely to be able to do a British graduate degree in two years. Most students who have or are about to complete an undergraduate degree in the United States usually opt for a second undergraduate degree in Britain. In many ways British undergraduate degrees are more like master's degrees in the United States since native students do specific preparation in secondary school for the university. Matriculation through the subsequent undergraduate program is very focused on the major from the very beginning and lasts three years.

Applicants are expected to have corresponded with their university choices. Information about British universities can be obtained from the following publications: *Commonwealth Universities Yearbook*, *British Universities Guide to Graduate Study*, *Current Research in Britain*, and, *Study in Britain*, which is free and available from the Reference Division of the British Information Services, 845 Third Avenue, New York, NY 10022.

In order to write the "Proposed Academic Programme" section of the application, you should have selected a degree program and possess specific data about that program. The more focused the area and the more specific you can be about which faculty you will study under, the better the chances of winning are. This all means that corresponding with the university, college, and faculty is key to success.

The selection committee is looking for people who give evidence they will become involved in activities outside of their academic interests. Specific types of outside interests and potential activities should be documented in the narrative. Certainly a sincere, demonstrated appreciation of British culture and a desire to learn more about the people and history are crucial. Students, for example, are expected to take their vacations in Britain in order to become more familiar with the society. Enthusiasm for things British must be conveyed in the application.

Since the Marshall is concerned about an applicant's ability to join in non-academic activities, you might ask one of your references to write about your interaction in and enthusiasm for on-campus and off-campus activities as well as your academic preparedness.

Students who make the short list are asked to participate in an interview at the regional Consulate-General through which their application was processed. If a practice interview is available at your college, you should take advantage of it. You should be prepared to expand in detail upon your proposed course of study and to answer tough questions about the project from a committee member in the field. In addition, you should be able to demonstrate knowledge of Great Britain and an enthusiasm for learning more about the culture. The odds of winning a Marshall if invited to be interviewed are around 50/50.

2. CSC-PRC Graduate Study/Dissertation Research in China[2]

Administrative Agency: Committee on Scholarly Communication with China.

Address: Committee on Scholarly Communication with China
1055 Thomas Jefferson Street NW
Suite 2013
Washington, DC 20007
Phone: 202-337-1250

Deadline: Mid-October.

Award Notification: March.

Number of Awards: 20 per competition.

Average Number of Applicants: 60 per competition.

---

2. Based on the 1994–1995 CSCC Exchange Programs with China, The Committee on Scholarly Exchange with China (CSCC).

Award Amount: Room and board allowance; tuition and fees if any; travel to China and within China. The award provides no support for dependents.

Application Form: Applicants should check the international office, study abroad office, or Asian languages department or write to the above address.

Purpose of Grant/Fellowship and Restrictions: The award is intended to support graduate students in the humanities and social science who wish to study or do research in the People's Republic of China. Students may apply in the General Advanced Study (GAS) category, which supports students who are enrolled in classes as well as, in some cases, those undertaking individual study under the direction of a faculty member. A second application category is the Senior Advanced Study (SAS) level, in which advanced research, usually for a dissertation, is undertaken. Applicants may apply in only one category.

Length of Award: One 11-month academic year, with a possible extension.

Applicant Eligibility: An applicant must be a U.S. citizen or U.S. permanent resident with a bachelor's degree who has had three years of Chinese language study before application and is willing to stay 11 months in China (September–July).

General Application Requirements: A completed application form, which includes: a six-page or less double-spaced study or research plan; official transcripts; statement of Chinese language courses; three references from scholars in the field. Those who pass the first level of scrutiny must take a language exam and interview.

Advanced language skills are fundamental to success in this competition.

Application Comments and Advice: Preference is given to students who have had experience in a Chinese language setting. Preference is also given to students working on focused, advanced research projects. This fellowship is not for language study.

The GAS and SAS categories require a knowledge of the possibilities for research or study that are available in China; so advanced preparation for this competition is crucial. Certainly the more contacts you have made the better, especially in the dissertation research area.

Applicants in either area should provide compelling evidence that study or research in China is absolutely necessary. This usually entails giving specific evidence that substantiates that all avenues and resources in this country have been exhausted.

Advanced research applicants should provide clear and attainable objectives, a well-articulated methodology, and a specific description of resources to be tapped in China. Again, contacts in China go a long way in assuring reviewers that the project is indeed feasible.

Working with an advisor who has extensive experience in China will help you establish what is possible and what is not. Support from such a scholar enhances the possibility of an award. References are important in any competition, but they must be especially enthusiastic for work in a country where the systems are complex and foreigners are often viewed with suspicion.

3. Deutscher Akademischer AustauschDienst Grants for Study and Research in Germany[3]

The focus of this description is the Annual Grant for Study and Research, which is available to full-time enrolled undergraduates and master's and doctoral students interested in study and research in Germany in any field. Some information is also provided here about other DAAD opportunities.

Administrative Agency: German Academic Exchange Service.

Address: German Academic Exchange Service
950 Third Avenue, 19th Floor
New York, NY 10022
Phone: 212-758-3223

Deadline: Early November for Annual Study and Research Grants. Other DAAD opportunities described below have a variety of deadlines.

Award Notification: Mid-March.

Award Amount: Monthly stipend of DM 1,075 or DM 1,555, depending on academic level; one-time baggage, book, and start-up stipend; round-trip plane ticket; health and accident insurance policy.

3. Based on the 1993 DAAD, German Academic Exchange Service.

Application Form: The Fulbright advisor, study abroad office, or international office should have applications. Application for the Annual Research and Study Grant must be done through the campus officer.

Purpose of Grant/Fellowship and Restrictions: DAAD offers a number of grant opportunities. The idea is to promote better academic international relations through exchanges of students, faculty, and professionals. Programs are offered to undergraduate and graduate students in a variety of fields to improve language skills and to do academic research in Germany. A summer program for doctoral students is held at the University of California at Berkeley, and several language improvement courses are offered during the summer in Germany. In addition to the regular doctoral research opportunity in Germany, there are special programs devoted to research in German Jewry and postwar topics and an opportunity to study contemporary German literature at Washington University in St. Louis.

Length of Award: Ten months.

Applicant Eligibility: An applicant must be a U.S. citizen, not more than 31 years of age by the application deadline, who is enrolled fulltime at a DAAD-sanctioned university and has a research project, and German language skills sufficient to carry out the proposal. Preference is given to students who have been invited to study or do research at a German university, institution, or laboratory.

Application Requirements: Application form; passport photos; curriculum vitae; project description in English and, for those in German language and literature, history, philosophy, or theology, a description in German; two letters of recommendation from professors; certificate of language ability; and official transcripts. Applications must be made through DAAD program officers on campus.

Some DAAD fellowships require simultaneous application to Fulbright (IIE).

Application Comments and Advice: Previous study or research in Germany does not inhibit being selected for a DAAD. Key to this grant is an established contact, preferably with a faculty member, at a German university, institute, or laboratory with whom you will study or conduct research. It is important to start working on contacts during the spring and summer prior to the fall application deadline. Written invitations and acceptances for university study are crucial to being selected for a

DAAD grant. Faculty in German departments should be very helpful in making recommendations about German university and faculty contacts; the DAAD program officer might also be helpful in this area. On some campuses the application process is similar to that conducted for IIE Fulbrights in that the applicant goes through an on-campus interview with a faculty committee. The committee's recommendations are forwarded to DAAD as part of the application package.

4. Fulbright (IIE) Grants for Study, Research, and Teaching Abroad[4]

Administrative Agency: Institute of International Education.

Address: IIE
U.S. Student Programs Division
809 United Nations Plaza
New York, NY 10017-3580
Phone: 212-984-5330

Deadline: On-campus deadlines in mid- to late September; at large applications in late October.

Award Notification: From January through June depending upon the country.

Number of Awards: 900 per competition.

Average Number of Applicants: 4,000 per competition.

Award Amount: Varies according to country. The award usually includes transportation, tuition, book and research allowances, and room and board support.

Application Form: Applications for the on-campus competition can be obtained through the Fulbright officer; at-large applicants (those not applying through a college or university campus but directly to IIE) should contact IIE at above address.

Purpose of Grant/Fellowship and Restrictions: The purpose of the award is to promote better relations with other nations. Recent college graduates, graduate students at all levels, artists, and young professionals in

4. Based on the 1995–1996 Fulbright Grants and other Grants for Graduate Study Abroad, Institute of International Education.

any field may study, do research, or teach abroad. The program is most interested in applicants who have not had extensive experiences in another country.

Length of Award: Six months to a year, usually a year.

Applicant Eligibility: Applicants must be U.S. citizens at the time of application, have a bachelor's degree prior to going abroad (although some exceptions are possible in the arts or where other experience is sufficient) and language skills that are sufficient to carry out the proposed study or research, and be in good health. MD's must have a degree at time of application; applicants may hold a JD; applicants to Germany under the DAAD program may have a PhD.

Application Requirements: Completed application in a single package; official transcripts; and language evaluation form. In addition, creative and performing artists should submit a supplemental packet of materials germane to their specialty; this may include slides, photographs, portfolios, films, videotapes, or tape recordings.

An at-large category is available for applicants who are no longer on a college or university campus. At-large candidates should apply directly to IIE.

Applicants who participate in an on-campus program must work with the Fulbright officer. The on-campus process includes an interview with faculty members and an evaluation and rating from the Faculty Fulbright Committee. IIE provides a 80-page booklet that describes the opportunities for study, research, and teaching in each country. You should get a booklet early in the springh (15 months prior to planned departure abroad) to see if the country in which you are interested offers the opportunity you seek. Only five countries, for example, offer opportunities to teach English. Some countries have special restrictions; Albania prefers unmarried candidates; Israel seeks postdoctoral applicants who are 35 years of age or under; Bulgaria will consider people only in the humanities, physical sciences, or social sciences. And on it goes.

Application Comments and Advice: Application may be made to only one country. Early contact in the spring before fall application with the on-campus Fulbright advisor is basic. Contacts with institutions overseas should be made prior to application, especially if you are doing research or seeking further education at a university. Those who wish to teach English in Belgium/Luxembourg, France, Germany, Korea, or Taiwan need not make prior contacts, but since positions in specific cities at certain schools may be requested by the applicant, it is best to have figured out the possibilities well in advance. Letters of invitation from archives or from scholars willing to assist or admission to a university carries a lot of weight in the selection process.

The applications are judged on how much the project will promote good will among nations; how well the project matches a country's interests; and the ratio of applications to opportunities (the odds are provided in the booklet). When all things are equal, preference is given to veterans or to candidates who have spent less time abroad.

Four elements are crucial to the application: the Statement of Proposed Study or Research, your curriculum vitae, the Foreign Language Report, and the on-campus interview. Other elements such as references are also important, but the above will make or break the application.

The key request in the Statement of Proposed Study or Research is for a justification of why the study/research or teaching must be done in the chosen country. This means that you must have given very careful consideration to choosing the country and provide specific reasons why what is proposed cannot be done elsewhere. Perhaps crucial papers for your dissertation project are located in a Berlin archives or the specific style of painting you want to learn is taught only at an English school. Reasons should be carefully spelled out. *A key to being selected is that whatever is proposed should promote mutual understanding between the United States and the chosen country.* That idea should be communicated in the narrative.

Of second importance is a request for the outline of a plan that can reasonably be completed abroad within the time frame. Most applicants imagine that they can do more than they can in a year. Faculty who have studied or done research abroad can be very helpful.

The curriculum vitae is a second narrative, the aim of which is to allow the reviewers to get to know you as a person. It is important to center your intellectual development around family, educational, and cultural experiences. The intellectual interests that finally culminated in the plan described in the Statement of Proposed Study or Research should be emphasized. The two narratives should work together but not be repetitious.

It is very important that your language skills be good enough to support the plan you describe in the Statement. Check with a language department faculty member to see whether your language skills are sufficient. If they are not, indicate in the Statement what you will do to improve those skills prior to your departure. That could include taking courses during the academic year; enrolling in special summer programs; or, for countries with a rarely taught language, arranging for special instruction upon arrival. (These special language training opportunities are often described in the booklet and are well worth repeating.) Every conceivable effort should be made to have the best language skills possible.

The Campus Committee Evaluation Form in the packet gives a sense of what kinds of data the interviewers will seek. The interviewers will have gotten most of the information from a prior reading of your completed application. Two areas, however, are not easily covered in the application: "knowledge of the host country" and "evaluation of impression candidate will make abroad as a citizen representing the United States" (which is a key element in the selection process). Be sure to know as much as possible about the chosen country, especially about current events. Fulbright is looking for people who are interested in and who care about citizens of other cultures; so it is important to reflect those types of concerns.

5. Fulbright-Hays (DOE) Dissertation Research in Area Studies in Non-Western Countries[5]

Administrative Agency: U.S. Department of Education.

Address: U.S. Department of Education
Center for International Education
400 Maryland Avenue SW
Washington, DC 20202-5331
Phone: 202-732-6061

Deadline: End of October.

Award Notification: Late March–early April.

Number of Awards: Up to 60 per competition.

Average Number of Applicants: 580 per competition.

Award Amount: Calculated by country. This is one of the few fellowships to offer very generous spouse and child support. It is possible for an awardee with a family of three additional dependents to receive over $50,000 for a year of support.

---

5. Based on the 1994–1995 Doctoral Dissertation Research Abroad Program (Fulbright-Hays), Center for International Education, U.S. Department of Education.

Application Form: Application *must* be made through a university. Applicants should check the graduate school or international studies office on campus.

Purpose of Grant/Fellowship and Restrictions: The award's intention is to provide dissertation research opportunities to students in modern foreign languages and area studies who wish to do research in non-Western European areas such as Africa, East Asia, Southeast Asia and the Pacific, South Asia, the Near East, Central Europe (Poland, the Czech Republic, Slovakia, Hungary, Albania, Rumania, the republics that were formerly part of Yugoslavia), the Baltic States and other new republics of the former Soviet Union, and the Western hemisphere. Area studies means "a program of comprehensive study of the aspects of society or societies, including the study of their geography, history, culture, economy, politics, international relations, and languages."

Length of Award: Six months to one year.

Applicant Eligibility: Applicants should be U.S. citizens, U.S. permanent residents, or residents of a trust territory who are graduate students in good standing at the dissertation stage when the fellowship period begins and plan careers in academia and who have sufficient language skills to carry out their research.

Application Requirements: A completed application, including: standard form 424, which is completed by the university (an institution may forward an unlimited number of individual student applications); general application information sheets, including a budget; a foreign language reference, three letters of reference; a curriculum vitae; and an essay not to exceed 10 typed, double-spaced pages.

For the most part, the budget is formulized according to an allotment allowed for each individual country. That information is at the end of the application.

Application Comments and Advice: The application contains a description of how evaluation points are assigned; this formula should be followed carefully.

Of the 100 points, 45 points are assigned to: project originality and quality of problems, questions, and hypotheses; demonstrated familiarity with research in the area; methodology; demonstrated use of U.S. resources; demonstrated need to go to the chosen country; the establishment of contacts in the chosen country; willingness to share the results, especially with the host country; the complete support and supervision of the dissertation advisor; and assurance that the project can reasonably be completed within the time period. In addition, it is advisable to weave into the narrative structure a sense of the significance of your research to the field. Agencies are most interested in funding research that has a substantive impact. The research significance information should go in the originality section. The best procedure when constructing the narrative is to write in exactly the same order in which information is requested. This leaves little doubt in reviewers' minds that the areas requested have been covered.

Another 45 points are assigned to your qualifications. These include: the quality of your academic record and its relevance to the project, your language skills, and evidence that you can conduct research abroad. Fulbright-Hays is enthusiastic about applicants who have had previous overseas experience—the more the better. Information will be evaluated by assessing your letters of reference, the courses you have taken, and your curriculum vitae. Letters of reference must be absolutely, unfailingly enthusiastic, especially from your dissertation advisor. The curriculum vitae is a good place to explain your research experiences abroad as well as to list your other grants and academic honors.

Finally, 10 points are assigned to program priorities in the fields of modern languages and area studies that are described in the application package.

It is expected that applicants who do not win an award or who are named as alternatives will reapply. The Department makes evaluators' comments available upon written request and encourages applicants to retrieve this information. Since Fulbright-Hays also offers fellowships to faculty scholars, it is a good idea to write for remarks since future application either as a student or faculty scholar is likely.

Do not neglect to have an examination by a physician; failure to do so will jeopardize the application.

6. International Research and Exchange (IREX) Grants for Central and Eastern Europe, the former Soviet Union, and Mongolia[6]

Administrative Agency: International Research and Exchange Grants.

6. Based on the 1993–1994 Grant Opportunities for U.S. Scholars, International Research and Exchange Board.

Address: IREX
1616 H Street NW
Washington, DC 20006
Phone: 202-628-8188

Deadline: Early November for Individual Advanced Research Opportunities; early November for On-Site Language Training; early November for the Slavic Studies Seminar; and mid-December for the Summer Language Program for College and University Instructors of Languages.

Award Notification: Variable according to program.

Number of Awards: 47 per competition for Individual Advanced Research Opportunities; 3 for On-Site Language Training; 50 for the Short-term Travel Grant; 8 for the Slavic Studies Seminar; and 20 for the Summer Language Program.

Average Number of Applicants: 105 per competition for Individual Advanced Research Opportunities; 10 for On-Site Language Training; and 200 for the Short-term Travel Grant.

Award Amount: Variable according to program.

Application Form: Applicants should contact the Russian or Slavic languages department or the international office on campus, or write to the address above.

Purpose of Grant/Fellowship and Restrictions: IREX aims to guarantee access to resources in Central and Eastern Europe for scholarly research by pre- and postdoctoral academics in social science and the humanities.
   Individual Research Opportunities support two to twelve months of research in Albania, Bulgaria, the Czech Republic, Slovakia, Hungary, Poland, Romania, the former Yugoslav Republics, the States of the former Soviet Union, Mongolia. Travel, stipend, research allowances.
   On-Site Language Training in Central and Eastern Europe are grants to the same areas for two to twelve months for the purpose of improving language skills. It includes travel and stipend grants.
   The **Slavic Studies Seminar** grants are for one-month fellowships to attend a language and literature enhancement seminar in Bulgaria. Travel, room and board, and fees are covered.

The *Summer Language Program for College and University Instructors of Languages of the States of the Former Soviet Region* supports seven weeks of very advanced language training at a university in Russia. The award covers travel, room and board, and fees.

Length of Award: See the descriptions under Purpose of Grant/Fellowship and Restrictions.

Applicant Eligibility: An applicant should be a U.S. citizen or U.S. permanent resident with advanced language skills who is enrolled full time in an academic program as a master's or doctoral student. Applicants in modern foreign languages and area studies only are required to apply simultaneously for any Department of Education grants that are appropriate (such as the Fulbright-Hays).

7. Japanese Government (Monbusho) Scholarships for Research Students[7]

Administrative Agency: Consulate General of Japan.

Address: Consulate General of Japan
911 Main, 2519 Commerce Tower
Kansas City, MO 64105-2076
Phone: 816-471-0111
Or contact the nearest Japanese Consulate General.

Deadline: Early in fall for the application and mid-fall for the language examination and interview. Precise date depends on district rules.

Award Notification: January.

Number of Awards: 40 per competition.

Average Number of Applicants: Hard to estimate because the competition is held in 15 districts. The Kansas City district, for example, usually has 5–6 applications, but the number can vary across districts.

Award Amount: About $1,725 per month, plus transportation, an arrival allowance, and partial medical expenses.

7. Based on the 1994 Japanese Government (Monbusho) Scholarships for Research Studies, Consulate General of Japan in Kansas City, MO.

Application Form: Applicants should check with their Japanese language department or international studies office or write to the above address.

Purpose of Grant/Fellowship and Restrictions: The award is intended to provide research opportunities to American students in all fields. Researchers will be assigned by the Japanese Ministry of Education to a university as a non-degree affiliate.

Length of Award: Eighteen months to two years.

Applicant Eligibility: Applicants should be U.S. citizens of 34 years of age or under; advanced Japanese language ability; in good mental and physical health, and should have a bachelor's degree awarded prior to beginning of fellowship period.

Application Requirements: A completed application form, including a 500-word proposed plan of research; a recent passport photograph; official transcripts; medical certification; letters of recommendation; a photocopy of the applicant's college diploma; a letter of invitation from a Japanese faculty member; a language examination; and an interview at the consulate-general in the application district. Artists should provide a sample of their work.

The competition is carried out through fifteen districts in the United States. Each applicant must go to the district consulate general office in the fall for a language examination and an interview.

Application Comments and Advice: The quality of your proposed plan of research, your level of language skills, and your interview are the primary criteria for selection. A proposal can be written with or without research contacts in Japan, but preference is given to applicants who have made prior contacts and received invitations to do research or study. Language skills should be advanced.

The interview is an important and mandatory part of the process. Applicants should be able to answer questions about the feasibility of their research within the time frame requested as well as present compelling reasons for going to Japan.

The proposed plan of research has two parts, which cover what research is to be done and how it is to be conducted. The second section clearly requires that you demonstrate specific familiarity with the resources available in Japan. The section can be written in Japanese or English.

8. Rhodes Scholarships to Oxford University in Great Britain[8]

Administrative Agency: The Rhodes Trust.

Address: Professor David Alexander
American Secretary of the Rhodes Scholarships
Pomona College
Claremont, CA 91711-6305

Deadline: Mid-October.

Award Notification: December.

Number of Awards: 32 per competition.

Award Amount: Tuition and other costs at Oxford, £6,066 per year allowance, and travel expenses to and from Oxford.

Application Form: Applicants should check with the undergraduate or graduate school administrative office (most institutions will have a faculty administrator and a committee) or write to the address above.

Purpose of Grant/Fellowship and Restrictions: The purpose of the award is to provide study opportunities for a second undergraduate or a graduate degree at Oxford University for scholars who demonstrate potential for leadership.

Length of Award: Minimum of two years and maximum of three years (under special conditions).

Applicant Eligibility: Applicants should be U.S. citizens between the ages of 18 and 24, unmarried, who have completed a bachelor's degree prior to the beginning of the Rhodes scholarship (October).

Application Requirements: A completed application form; official transcripts; a professional photograph (like a passport photo); a copy of a birth certificate; up to eight letters of reference; a medical examination; a resume of college activities and honors; and an essay of 1,000 words or less on the proposed plan of study.
　　Leadership abilities are a high priority in this competition and are

8. Based on the Rhodes Scholarships, September 1992, The Rhodes Trust.

judged on evidence of leadership experience plus participation in sports.

Application Comments and Advice: Of special importance to selection is a narrative description of your academic as well as non-academic interests; the narrative is not to exceed 1,000 words. The statement should combine a focused interest in an academic area with a sense of future goals based on past interests. In the best of all worlds, a Rhodes scholar has a big worldly vision of his or her capabilities to lead. President Clinton is a perfect Rhodes example. The ability to interact well with all kinds of people and the vigor to undertake a myriad of projects both academic and non-academic (the English way is to pursue clubs, hobbies, and sports with the same energy as academics) is very important. If one can visualize two years at Oxford as being the springboard to a very specific future, all the better. A reminder of your athletic enthusiasm must appear somewhere in the narrative.

Two interviews are possible with a Rhodes. The first can occur at a state level, the second at a district level. Some colleges and universities offer candidates who are called for interviews a practice interview; if this is available, you should take advantage of it. Since Rhodes is looking for the intelligent, energetic, well-rounded leader, ability to interact comfortably with a group of people is important. Mix humor with seriousness and expect to speak eloquently about your future goals and to demonstrate a familiarity with Oxford (the system as it differs from ours) and an understanding and enthusiasm for English culture and history.

With regard to references, Rhodes is looking for testimonials from a diverse group of people. Academic endorsements are important, but so are words of high praise about your ability to lead and work well with people, your athletic competence, and your high moral character and extraordinary energy. Letters from such people as professors, deans or directors of student activities or associations, directors of volunteer agencies one might have worked for, coaches, religious leaders, and employers should be sought. All these people should be willing to express absolute enthusiasm for you as gained from a very close perspective.

9. Rotary Foundation Academic-Year Ambassadorial Scholarships[9]

Administrative Agency: Rotary Foundation of Rotary International.

9. Based on the 1994–1995 Rotary Foundation Scholarship Application and Information Packet, The Rotary Foundation of Rotary International.

Address: Rotary Foundation
One Rotary Center
1560 Sherman Avenue
Evanston, IL 60201
Phone: 708-866-3000
Or contact the Rotary Club in the area of home or college for information about local competition rules and deadlines.

Deadline: Varies according to club and region. It would be wise to start investigating opportunities in March some 18 months prior to departure abroad.

Award Notification: By January.

Number of Awards: 1,328 worldwide per competition.

Number of Applicants: Unknown, because applications are submitted to over 25,000 clubs in 184 countries. Each club may receive one or more applications. The local club then opts to recommend or not recommend their applicants to the district-level competition. No accurate records are kept regarding the initial number of applicants. Japan and the United States have the most applicants. Not every club has applicants every year.

Award Amount: $20,000, plus travel allowance.

Application Form: Applicants should check with the Rotary Club through which application is to be made. Many university and college administrative offices also have applications on hand.

Purpose of Grant/Fellowship and Restrictions: The award's objective is to promote international goodwill and help improve international relations in the parts of the world where there are Rotary Clubs. Rotary scholars are expected to interact with Rotarians in the country in which they study. There are five types of grants offered: journalism; teachers of handicapped people; vocational study; undergraduates; graduate study. All scholarships are for study abroad, but this description focuses on Academic-Year Ambassadorial Scholarships for graduate study. Graduate scholarships are for people who have received a bachelor's degree or the equivalent and wish to study abroad for one academic year in any field.

Length of Award: One academic year.

Applicant Eligibility: An applicant must be a citizen of a country in which there is a Rotary Club; study must be done in a country or territory in which there is a Rotary Club; and language skills must be sufficient to study and live in the chosen country. Rotarians or employees of Rotary or their spouses or lineal descendants (a child or grandchild by blood or legal adoption) are ineligible, as are spouses of lineal descendants or ancestors (parent or grandparent by blood) of Rotarians or Rotary employees.

Application Requirements: A completed application form, consisting of several essays, a language ability form, two recommendation forms, and transcripts.

Application must be made through a local Rotary Club. Relatives of Rotarians or Rotary employees are ineligible.

Application Comments and Advice: Persistence is important in applying for a Rotary. Since every club has its own competition rules, candidates must be willing to seek out information and nudge local Rotarians into endorsing an application. This might entail going to a local Rotary lunch and explaining why study abroad is important. The ability to speak publicly and willingness to do so are crucial. It is important to Rotary that their scholars be good ambassadors; so a demonstrated ability to interact with their club members both in the United States and abroad is key to winning an award.

The application requests essays that entail 3 elements.

(1) You must provide a description of your academic strengths and weaknesses, work experiences, career goals, and significant life events. Any weaknesses described should be those that you have overcome—perhaps a bad grade in your freshman year attributable to initial adjustment to college life—but not a current condition. If there are no real glaring weaknesses in your academic record, do not present any; in other words, do not feel obliged to describe a weakness unless it can somehow be turned into a plus.

(2) You must provide a statement about your proposed field of study, its relationship to future goals as described in (1), and a rationale for picking the country (two may be listed) and institution (five may be listed) in which your study is to be undertaken. Thus, before application is made, you must thoroughly research universities overseas. Information about institutions abroad should be available in the campus library or the international or study abroad offices or by writing for information from universities abroad. You are responsible for gaining admission to your chosen place of study.

It is crucial to write the purpose of study essay with a sense of focus and commitment to your field of study. It is also important to indicate why study in the country is important. Going abroad just to get away is not enough. Perhaps a particular educational opportunity is available in only that country. Learning Finnish silversmithing, for example, is best done in Finland. The odds of winning an award are heightened when a compelling reason for going to a particular country and a particular program are convincingly presented.

(3) Under certain conditions, a translation of the essays into a second language other than English is required.

At least one interview will be conducted by Rotary personnel. Applicants need to be comfortable interacting in a group. Every interviewee should know as much about the country of application as possible, including current and historical events. An appreciation of the foreign culture is important because Rotary is interested in improving international relations. A presentation to the interviewing group about your proposed plan of study may also be part of the process.

10. Social Science Research Council Fellowships[10]

The Social Science Research Council offers a variety of opportunities to do predissertation and dissertation field research abroad. Since application rules vary for each type of award, the format for describing SSRC fellowships below includes general descriptions of the two types of fellowships. Table 2 gives a listing of opportunities by geographic area. Detailed information is available from SSRC in a 60-page booklet. SSRC also publishes a very good booklet on proposal writing.

Administrative Agency: Social Science Research Council.

Address: SSRC
605 Third Avenue
New York, NY 10158
Phone: 212-661-0280

Purpose of Grant/Fellowship and Restrictions: In general, the Social Science Council fellowships aim to support graduate students, primarily at the predissertation and dissertation research levels. There are a few language training awards that fund students at all graduate levels. Social science fields not eligible are social work, clinical psychology, and education.

---

10. Based on the Social Science Research Council Fellowships and Grants for Training and Research for 1992–1993, Social Science Research Council.

Pre-dissertation fellowships are awarded to graduate students, primarily in the fields of economics, political science, and sociology, who are interested in getting area study training in a developing country. They are additionally offered in the geographic areas listed below.

TABLE 2. SSCR Grants

Geographic area	Types of funding available	Deadline
Africa (Sub-Saharan)	Predissertation Fellowships for Short Field Trips	Nov. 1
	Dissertation Fellowships	Nov. 1
	Agricultural Training Fellowships	TBA
China	Chiang Ching-kuo/JCCS Dissertation Fellowships	Dec. 1
Eastern Europe	Advanced Graduate Training Fellowships (year before dissertation)	Dec. 1
	Predissertation Travel Grants	March 1
	East European Language Training Grants (any level graduate)	Nov. 1
Japan	Fellowships for Dissertation Write-Up	Jan. 1
Korea	Dissertation Fellowships	Jan. 1
Latin America and the Caribbean	Dissertation Fellowships	Nov. 1
Near and Middle East	Dissertation Fellowships	Nov. 1
South Asia	Dissertation Fellowships	Nov. 1
Southeast Asia	Pre-dissertation Fellowships	Nov. 1
	Dissertation Fellowships	Nov. 1
Soviet Union and Its Successor States	Graduate Training Fellowships	Dec. 1
	Dissertation Fellowships	Dec. 1
Western Europe	Dissertation Fellowships	Nov. 1
	Berlin Program for Advanced German and European Studies	Feb. 1

Dissertation fellowships are available to students in the social sciences and humanities. To be eligible, students must be enrolled full time. Most programs have no citizenship requirements, but a few are restricted to U.S. citizens and U.S. permanent residents. Support is unusually for nine to eighteen months of field research. Travel, cost of living stipend, and research expenses are included.

Application Comments and Advice: See the general application advice at the beginning of this chapter.

Further Reading

Financial Resources for International Study: A Definitive Guide to Organizations Offering Awards for Overseas Study. Institute for International Education. Princeton, NJ: Peterson's Guides, 1989.

Chapter 5
Research Grants

This chapter presents general information and application writing advice for all the research grants for which a person may apply. It also describes in detail certain specific grant opportunities, namely:

1. American Museum of Natural History Research Grants
2. Explorers Club Grants for Graduate Students and Members of Expeditions
3. Geological Society of America Research Grants
4. Lindberg Grant (Technology and the Environment)
5. Oak Ridge Associated Universities Research Travel Grants for Research at U.S. Department of Energy Facilities
6. Phillips Fund Grants for Native American Studies
7. Presidential Library Research Grants
8. Sigma Xi Research Grants

Grants listed in this section are of interest to: junior and senior undergraduates, first- through fifth-year graduate students, and postdocs.

Fields funded by one or more of these grants: social sciences, sciences, humanities, and engineering.

Degree candidates funded by these grants: Bachelor's, master's, and doctoral.

General Information

The purpose of research grants is to support work on a specific project. The project may be in the exploratory, middle, or advanced stages. Research grants are available to purchase equipment and other supplies, to conduct surveys or experiments, to provide living support for the researcher, and to encourage travel to collections. Research grants are available to people at all levels including undergraduate, master's, and doctoral students in all fields; postdoctoral researchers; faculty; and independent scholars.

Finding research money often takes careful detective work. While well-known opportunities are listed on data bases and in grant listings, far more can be found through determined hunting. For example, organizations like the American Chemical Association, the American Economic Association, the American Society of Plant Taxonomy, the Geological Society of America, and the Society of Actuaries offer research grants within their scope of interest, but their opportunities are not widely advertised. Reading the journals in your discipline and contacting the associations and societies within your field of study are good ways to tap these funds.

Another place to look for research money is in non-academic, not-for-profit agencies, such as the Epilepsy Foundation, which encourage research in a specialty area by providing financial support. The best place to look for these research funds is in a publication entitled *The Encyclopedia of Associations*, which can be found in any large library, usually in the reference section. It lists almost every well-established not-for-profit organization in the United States.

Other sources of funds, about which information is not always easily accessible, are local, state, or regional agencies and foundations that are too small to be noticed by the large databases and grant lists. Somewhere in every state is an organization that gathers information about these resources. State or city libraries can usually identify these sources.

State government can also be a source of research grant support. Many states publish a booklet describing what they fund. Sometimes it may take a series of phone calls to various state agencies to establish whether research money is available. State money is typically earmarked for research in conservation, historic preservation, education, environmental improvement, social welfare, public policy, and agriculture, as well as in other areas.

Museums, archives, and libraries are three other sources of unadvertised research money. Because organizations are eager to have scholars utilize their resources, they often set aside money for the purpose of bringing people in to study their collections, manuscripts, documents, or books. When looking for this sort of support, first determine where data or artifacts are located and then contact the institution to see whether money is available for travel to the collections and, if so, how one applies. The more famous of these research grants, such as those offered by the Presidential Libraries discussed below, may be well known, but there are many, many more that are not listed anywhere and take determination and perseverance to secure.

General Application Advice

1. **Hunt in out-of-the-way places.** Use the resources mentioned above to look for opportunities.

2. **When a grant opportunity seems to fit your project but the organization's information is not clear enough about what is specifically supported, call the agency.** Sometimes local and regional funding sources will indicate broad, general fields of interest such as "education" or "social welfare." A call is needed to see what the specific support focus entails and whether students are eligible to apply.

3. **When writing a research grant proposal be sure to indicate the problem to be solved (or question to be answered), how the problem is to be solved (or question is to be answered), what the significance of the research will be to the field, and who is likely to benefit from the information.** Research must be seen as important beyond the needs of the researcher to be worthy of financial consideration.

4. **If you are requesting money to support part of a project, be sure to frame that part within the context of the larger research.** The big picture goes a long way in explaining the smaller project.

5. **Carefully research your financial needs and prepare a realistic budget.** Consult with faculty or research office personnel for help in this area if the application requirements seem too complicated.

6. **Sometimes money is only available through faculty or institutional sponsorship.** If this is the case, try to find a faculty member who will agree to act as the primary or principal investigator (PI).

7. **If a faculty PI is used, the project will probably have to go through the institution's sponsored projects office.** That means all kinds of signatures may be needed, and the budget will probably have to be reviewed outside of the department. Start early if that is the case.

Specific Grant Opportunities

The research grant opportunities listed in this section are just a sampling of what is available. Many, many more can be found through persistent research. All information, except the author's advice, is taken from the actual application packets, award announcements, and other documents written by administrative agencies, or on the basis of calls to the individual agencies. Every effort is made to use the same language as that on the application or to paraphrase or summarize that language. For ease of reading, quotation marks are used only to draw special attention to important application sections.

1. American Museum of Natural History Research Grants[1]

Administrative Agency: American Museum of Natural History.

Address: Office of Grants and Fellowships
American Museum of Natural History
79 St. and Central Park West
New York, NY 10024
Phone: 212-769-5100.

Deadline: Mid-January for the Chapman Memorial Grants; mid-March for the Lerner-Gray Grants for Marine Research; and mid-February for the Roosevelt Memorial Grants. There is no deadline for the Collection Study Grants.

Award Notification: Early April for the Chapman Memorial Grants; mid-May for the Lerner-Gray Grants; early April for the Roosevelt Memorial Grants; and 2 months after application submission for the Collection Study Grants.

Number of Awards: 200 per competition for all categories.

Award Amount: $200–$1,000 for the Chapman, Roosevelt, and Lerner-Gray Grants, with the average being $700. In some cases, awards may range between $1,000 and $2,000. Collection Study Grants are no more than $400.

Application Form: Applications may be available in geosciences, anthropology, or biological sciences departments, or by writing to address above.

Purpose of Grant/Fellowship and Restrictions: These short-term awards are designed to support advanced master's or doctoral students and postdoctoral fellows in their research. With the exception of the Collection Study Grants, the work need not be done at the Museum.

  Frank M. Chapman Memorial Grants are for research in ornithology.

1. Based on the 1993–1994 Grants and Fellowships of the American Museum of Natural History, American Museum of Natural History.

Lerner-Gray Grants for Marine Research support projects related to systematics, evolution, ecology, and field-oriented behavioral research in botany and biochemistry.

Theodore Roosevelt Memorial Grants are for research on wildlife conservation or the natural history of North American fauna. Projects should be compatible with the Museum's activities in these areas.

Collection Study Grants support travel to the Museum to study collections in the fields of vertebrate zoology, invertebrate zoology, paleozoology, anthropology, and mineral sciences.

Applicant Eligibility: The applicant must be an advanced graduate student or a postdoctoral fellow connected to an appropriate institution.

Application Requirements: An application, including requests for the name of the applicant's research advisor, an itemized budget, and a description of the project. The Chapman, Roosevelt or Lerner-Gray applications also require two letters of reference.

Application Comments and Advice: Collection Study Grant applicants should first contact the Museum and talk to a staff member to make sure that a trip to the Museum makes sense. This is an application requirement. The project description requests a detailing of the collection(s) to be studied, the name of the person on the Museum staff with whom the applicant will be working, and the significance of the project.

The Chapman, Roosevelt, and Lerner-Gray application project description requests do not detail what is wanted, but you should include a brief description of the project, the research plan (including methodology and time frames), the location of the project, the significance of the research, the contribution to science that will result from the research, and the project's relevance to the Museum's activities.

2. Explorers Club Grants for Graduate Students and Members of Expeditions[2]

Administrative Agency: Explorers Fund of the Explorers Club.

Address: The Explorers Club
46 East 70th Street
New York, NY 10021
Phone: 212-628-8383

---

2. Based on the 1994 Explorers Club Exploration Fund Grant Application, Explorers Club.

Deadline: End of January.

Award Notification: May.

Number of Awards: 30 per competition.

Award Amount: Up to $1,200.

Application Form: Applicants should check with the anthropology, archaeology, biology, or environmental sciences departments or write to address above.

Purpose of Grant/Fellowship and Restrictions: The Explorers Club is interested in supporting graduate students in exploration, field research, and expedition participation "to broaden our knowledge of the universe." Students at any stage of a master's and doctoral degree programs are eligible to apply. Students in the field of anthropology, archaeology, biology, and the environmental sciences are the most likely to receive awards, although there are no articulated field restrictions.

In addition to the graduate student awards, the Explorers Club has a youth activities program that funds approximately 60 high school and college students to pursue activities similar to those described above. The deadline for that program is usually earlier.

Applicant Eligibility: Applicants must have a worthy scientific project.

Application Requirements: A brief project description and budget; references.

Application Comments and Advice: The application is fairly simple and straightforward. You must describe your project in 50 words or less, provide the names of three people who may be contacted about the project, and include a budget and a description of the expedition you have been accepted on or with which you are trying to affiliate. Proposals are judged on their scientific and practical merits. In other words, the project must be scientifically sound and feasible. References should attest to these two requirements.

It is most important to secure a place on an expedition, dig, or other organized research project before applying for support. The tendency is to give awards to those students who have confirmation of research arrangements. Certainly use the leader of your research group as a reference to confirm your acceptance to the project team.

If the month of May comes and goes and no word has been forth-coming from the Club, call to see if the awards have been made. The Club can be a bit disorganized in providing information and sending checks in a timely manner. My son's check came a month after he had completed his research in Greece. The Club, however, is a wonderful source of small grants for worthy projects.

3. Geological Society of America Research Grants[3]

Administrative Agency: The Geological Society of America.

Address: Geological Society of America
3300 Penrose Place
P.O. Box 9140
Boulder, CO 80301
Phone: 303-447-2020, ext. 137

Deadline: Mid-February.

Award Notification: Mid-April.

Number of Awards: 200–250 per competition.

Average Number of Applicants: 580 per competition.

Award Amount: Highest award around $2,500; average award around $1,300. Research is usually expected to be done in the field and rarely at the university. There are clearly drawn guidelines about what the money can be used for. Tuition is not allowable, but most justifiable expenses related to field work are fundable.

Application Form: Applicants should check with the geology or earth and planetary sciences departments on campus, or write to the address above.

Purpose of Grant/Fellowship and Restrictions: The Society aims to give support to master's and doctoral students in the geosciences enrolled in programs in the United States, Canada, Mexico, and Central America. The expectation is that awards will be used to support field work.

3. Based on the 1993–1994 Geological Society of America Research Grants Program, Geological Society of American.

Areas of support include paleontology, sedimentology and stratigraphy, structure and tectonics, igneous and metamorphic petrology, economic geology (including hydrocarbons), quaternary geology and geomorphology, geophysics, hydrogeology, geochemistry, environmental geology, engineering geology, and other fields in the geosciences.

Length of Award: Depends on plan submitted.

Applicant Eligibility: Applicants must be enrolled in a university in North or Central America.

Application Requirements: Completed application, which includes 2 letters of reference from current program faculty.

Application Comments and Advice: The information/application packet supplied by the Geological Society of America is straightforward, uncomplicated, and full of good advice. The advice found in the packet is so good that those who follow it closely have an excellent chance of winning an award. Applicants are encouraged to construct a project that presents a problem and proposes a solution that is interesting enough to seize the imagination of the reviewers. In other words, you should not apply until you have an idea that is substantive and captivating and has the potential to contribute important information to the body of knowledge in the geosciences.

Applicants are told to put themselves in the shoes of the reviewers reviewing their work. It is probably a good idea to get a faculty member also to pretend to be a reviewer, particularly the faculty who will provide references.

The application is so well constructed in its requests that close attention to the form should produce a worthy proposal. Applicants are asked to state the hypothesis to be tested, explain why the research is of merit either to the discipline or to the region, describe a research plan, predict the duration of the plan, and draw up a budget. References are asked, among other things, to comment on the significance and practicality of the project.

It is important to note that while all evaluators will be professionals from the world of geosciences, they may not necessarily be experts within a particular subfield. This means overbearing use of jargon should be avoided.

The agency requests that applicants not call to seek the status of a submitted application.

4. Lindberg Grant (Technology and the Environment)[4]

Administrative Agency: The Charles A. Lindberg Fund, Inc.

Address: The Charles Lindberg Fund, Inc.
708 South 3rd Street
Suite 110
Minneapolis, MN 55415
Phone: 612-338-1703

Deadline: Mid-July.

Award Notification: Beginning of April of the following year.

Number of Awards: 10 per competition.

Average Number of Applicants: 200 per competition.

Award Amount: Up to $10,580 (the cost of building Lindberg's plane in 1927). Fundable items include computer time, supplies, and equipment, field work expense, reasonable secretarial and technical support, travel costs, and stipends.

Application Form: Applicants should write to the above address.

Purpose of Grant/Fellowship and Restrictions: Projects are sought that seek to establish a balance between the preservation of the human/ natural environment and advanced technology. Lindberg's vision was "to discern nature's essential wisdom and combine it with scientific knowledge." Projects from all fields are invited; however, these categories are specified: aviation/aerospace; agriculture; arts and humanities; biomedical research; conservation of natural resources; exploration; health and population sciences; intercultural communication; oceanography; waste disposal management; water resource management; and wildlife preservation.

Length of Award: Depends on the project.

Applicant Eligibility: All applicants are welcome.

4. Based on the 1994 Lindberg Grant Application, Charles Lindberg Fund.

Application Requirements: A completed application and letter of reference (endorser's report form). The application requires the submission of seven copies of everything.

Application Comments and Advice: The application requires a five to eight page delineation of your project, which includes a summary, review of the literature, budget, description of methodology, and description of the projected results and practical applications of the research. The summary should include a statement of the problem and the solution, your plan for getting to the solution, your anticipated results, the practical applications that can be anticipated, and how the project will improve the balance of technologic growth and environment preservation. The review of the literature is required and should include a statement about the originality of your project in relationship to the literature. A budget is also required. The methodology section should detail the plan for the solution and include a time frame for the work. The last section of the project delineation requires a discussion of the projected results and potential application of the information gained during the research.

Supporting information, including articles, photographs, and tapes, may be added to the application packet.

The most important factor to keep in mind when applying for a Lindberg is the purpose for the grant. It must involve modern technology and the environment. Sometimes it is difficult to be sure what kinds of projects fit into this category and the application process is complicated and time-consuming; so it is worth a call the agency to see if they consider your project of interest.

5. Oak Ridge Associated Universities Travel Grants for Research at U.S. Department of Energy Facilities[5]

Administrative Agency: Oak Ridge Associated Universities.

Address: Science/Engineering Education Division
Oak Ridge Associated Universities
P.O. Box 117
Oak Ridge, TN 37831-0117
Phone: 615-576-3000

---

5. Based on the 1993–1994 Oak Ridge Associated Universities Research Travel Opportunities, Oak Ridge Associated Universities.

Deadline: None. The award can be applied for at any time.

Award Notification: Six weeks after application.

Award Amount: A per diem amount of either $26 or $34, depending on where the research is done.

Application Form: Applications may be obtained from the science or engineering department or the research office on campus, or by writing to the address above.

Purpose of Grant/Fellowship and Restrictions: The travel fellowship is intended to give graduate students in the sciences and engineering an opportunity to do thesis research at the following U.S. Department of Energy research facilities: Atmospheric Turbulence and Diffusion Laboratory at Oak Ridge Associated Universities and Oak Ridge National Laboratory at Martin Marietta Energy Systems, Inc., which are both in Oak Ridge, TN; Center for Energy and Environment Research in Puerto Rico; Savannah River Ecology Laboratory and Savannah River Laboratory, both in Aiken, SC; Morgantown Energy Technology Center in Morgantown, WV; Pittsburgh Energy Technology Center in Pittsburgh, PA.
A detailed description of the research areas available to visitors is found in a twelve-page flier included in the application.

Length of Award: For short-term visits of usually less than a week in duration.

Applicant Eligibility: Applicants should be graduate students who are U.S. citizens or U.S. permanent residents and are working on a thesis. There are some exceptions to this.

Application Requirements: A completed application form that includes endorsements from the major professor or graduate dean and the laboratory to be visited.

Application Comments and Advice: The only possibility of securing one of these awards is to establish contact with the research facility and get approval from whomever you will be working under there. The award is based on that premise plus evidence that you really need to go to the facility to get your work done.

6. Phillips Fund Grants for Native American Studies[6]

Administrative Agency: American Philosophical Society.

Address: Phillips Fund Grant
The Library: American Philosophical Society
151 South Independence Mall East
Philadelphia, PA 19106-3386
Phone: 215-440-3400

Deadline: Mid-March.

Number of Awards: 17 per competition.

Award Amount: Up to $1,500. Average award is $1,200. Support is given for travel, tapes, films, informants' fees, etc., but not for general maintenance.

Application Form: Applicants should check with the multicultural office or Native American studies center on campus or write to the address above.

Purpose of Grant/Fellowship and Restrictions: The aid is meant to support research in North American Indian linguistics and ethnohistory. "North American" is defined as the United States, the Northwest coast, and Alaska. Support is *not* provided for archaeology, ethnography, or psycholinguistics or the development of pedagogical materials.

Length of Award: One year.

Applicant Eligibility: The applicant should have a credible, scholarly project in Native American linguistics or ethnohistory.

Application Requirements: A completed application form and three letters of support received by the deadline. If an award is made and accepted, the Society requires the submission of a report subsequent to the conclusion of the research.

Application Comments and Advice: If you are applying in linguistics, you should be sure to supply sufficient information about your Native

6. Based on the 1993–1994 Fund Grants for Native American Studies, Phillips Fund.

American language abilities. If language skills are fundamental to your project, you should have a reference describe and verify your facility with one or more languages. Your references should all be familiar with the particular project for which funding is requested.

If you need permission to visit a particular group or site, an invitation from that group or permission from the site should be included within the application.

A description of the project is requested. Since the space allocated is sparse, a longer statement may and should be appended. The description should include a delineation of the problem to be solved (or question to be asked) and the plan for solving the problem (or answering the question), which should include methodology and the significance of the project.

Another section asks that you list the research location, time schedules, types of assistance required, materials to be used or collected, and so on.

7. Presidential Library Research Grants[7]

This section provides information on eight libraries: Eisenhower, Ford, Hoover, Johnson, Kennedy, Reagan, Roosevelt, and Truman. The Nixon papers have been seized by the government and are not at the Nixon Library. The Jimmy Carter Library offers no grant money. All but the Nixon Library are established as private, non-governmental entities.

Administrative Agency: Office of Presidential Libraries (for basic information about Presidential Libraries only).

Address: Office of Presidential Libraries
       National Archive, Room 104
       Seventh and Pennsylvania Avenue NW
       Washington, DC 20408
       Phone: 202-501-5700
For addresses of individual library programs, see the appropriate program descriptions below.

Application Form: For all these grants, applicants should check with their on-campus history, American studies, or political science programs or write to the address(es) listed below.

---

7. Based on the 1993–1995 Information Packets from the Presidential Libraries.

Applicant Eligibility: Master's and doctoral students, postdocs, and established scholars are eligible to apply for Presidential Library Grants.

Application Comments and Advice: The first item of importance is to make sure the particular library has what you need. Once your research has been mapped out, it makes sense to call one or more of the libraries to see if a curator can locate the desired documents. In most cases, a contact with a staff member is a prerequisite to funding. Sometimes a library will not have a precise list of everything in a collection, but they will certainly know the substance of their holdings. It usually is possible to get documents microfilmed or copied and sent. Visiting should be done only when it is necessary to view a great many items.

A. Eisenhower World Affairs Institute

Address: Eisenhower World Affairs Institute
Abilene Travel Grants Program
918 16th Street NW
Washington, DC 20026
Phone: 202-223-6710
This grant is not administered through the library but from the Eisenhower Institute in Washington. It is still important to discuss the holdings and the project with an archivist at the library. The phone number in Abilene is 913-263-4751.

Deadline: Late February; late September.

Purpose of Grant/Fellowship and Restrictions: Support is provided for travel to the Eisenhower Library in Abilene, Kansas. In addition to research concerning Dwight Eisenhower, his family and associates, and his career and presidential administration, the Library encourages research in 1950s topics affected by the Eisenhower years. These topics include international and domestic economics, civil rights, space exploration, superpower relations, computer technology, and nuclear power and weaponry. In addition, the Library staff reports that many important papers have recently been declassified and are available for study.

General Application Requirements: A curriculum vitae, research plan, permission to use the holdings, publication plans, research timetable, budget, data about other grants applied for, and letter(s) of support.

Application Comments and Advice: A Library staff member should be contacted to ascertain the holdings available, check project feasibility, and to gain permission to use the archives.

B. Gerald R. Ford Library

Address: Gerald R. Ford Library
Grants Coordinator
1000 Beal Avenue
Ann Arbor, MI 48109-2114
Phone: 313-741-2218

Deadlines: Mid-September, mid-March.

Award Notification: 6–8 weeks after the deadline.

Number of Awards: Around 15 per year.

Award Amount: Up to $2,000. Support is provided for living, travel, photocopying expenses. ($20,000 a year is earmarked for travel to collections grants.)

Purpose of Grant/Fellowship and Restrictions: To do research in topics related to Gerald Ford.

Applicant Eligibility: Awards are available to doctoral candidates, established scholars, journalists, and others.

Application Comments and Advice: The Library provides a very good guide to the collections with a request for a grant application. It is also possible to retrieve documents by mail and to request a computer search of the archives. An archivist should be contacted for more information regarding these options.

C. Herbert Hoover Library

Address: Herbert Hoover Library
Parkside Drive
P.O. Box 696
West Branch, IA 52358
Phone: 319-643-5327

Deadline: Early March.

Award Notification: Early May.

Number of Awards: 20–25 per year.

Award Amount: Usual range is $500–$1,200. Requests for up to $10,000 may be made for extended graduate student or postdoctoral research. Per diem is $60; photocopying support up to $100 is possible.

Purpose of Grant/Fellowship and Restrictions: The grant is for travel to the Hoover Library in Iowa. Research of most interest to the Library is that which revolves around the lives of President Hoover, Lou Henry Hoover, their associates, and other public figures. The Library has 140 manuscripts in its collection. Projects that have a good chance of being published and are useful to educators and policy makers are most likely to win awards.

Application Comments and Advice: The archival staff should be consulted about project feasibility prior to application.

D. Lyndon Baines Johnson Library

Address: Lyndon Baines Johnson Library
        2313 Red River Street
        Austin, TX 78705
        Phone: 512-482-5137

Deadline: Late July for research done September through February; late January for research done March through August.

Award Notification: September for late July deadline; March for late January deadline.

Award Amount: Range is $500–$2,000. Per diem is $75.

Purpose of Grant/Fellowship and Restrictions: Support is awarded for travel to do research at the Library during the granting period.

Length of Award: Five months.

Application Comments and Advice: Potential applicants must contact the

Archives staff in order to receive information about the holdings and to determine project feasibility.

E. John F. Kennedy Library

Address: Chief Archivist
Kennedy Library
Columbia Point
Boston, MA 02125-3313
Phone: 617-929-4533

Purpose of Grant/Fellowship and Restrictions: The Kennedy Library is a private organization that invites students and scholars to submit applications for six different scholarships and one internship, all of which are described below.

The Marjorie Kovler Fellowship for research in the area of foreign intelligence and the presidency or a related topic. **Deadline** is mid March. **Award Notification** is late April. **Stipend** is $2,500. **Number of Awards** is one.

The Arthur M. Schlesinger, Jr. Fellowship for research in Latin American or Western Hemisphere history or policy studies during the Kennedy Administration or the period from the Roosevelt through the Kennedy presidencies. **Deadline** is mid August. **Award Notification** is mid October. **Stipend** is $5,000. **Number of Awards** is one or two.

The Abba Schwartz Fellowship is for research on immigration, naturalization, or refugee policy. **Deadline** is mid March. **Award Notification** is early May. **Stipend** is $3,100. **Number of Awards** is one.

The Theodore C. Sorensen Fellowship is for research on domestic policy, political journalism, polling, or press relations. **Deadline** is mid March. **Award Notification** is early May. **Stipend** is $3,600. **Number of Awards** is one.

Kennedy Research Grants are for research on any topic relating to the Kennedy period or requiring use of the holdings. Preference is given to Ph.D. dissertation research, research in recently opened or relatively unused collections and the preparation of recent dissertations for publication. **Deadline** is mid March for spring grants, mid August for fall grants. **Award Notification** is late April for spring grants, late October for fall grants. **Stipend** range of $500–$1,500. **Number of Awards** is 15–20.

Hemingway Research Grants are for research use of the Hemingway Collection. Preference is given to Ph.D. dissertation research. **Deadline** is mid March. **Award Notification** is late April. **Stipend** range is $200–$1000. **Number of Awards** is 5–10.

Paid Archival Internships are open to undergraduate and graduate students in the fields, primarily, of history, political science, English, journalism or communications. The internships are in the textual and audiovisual areas housed in the archives. Additional information is available by writing to the Intern Registrar or calling 617-929-4533.

Application Comments and Advice: The Library has recently opened previously sealed data for research by graduate students and scholars. A letter of inquiry or a call to the archivist is important in determining the scope of available holdings.

F. Ronald Reagan Library

Address: Ronald Reagan Library
        40 Presidential Drive
        Simi Valley, CA 93065
        Phone: 805-522-8444

The Reagan Library is considering a travel-to-collections grant program but has yet to establish one. Scholars should check periodically to learn the status of this opportunity.

G. Franklin D. Roosevelt Library

Address: Franklin D. Roosevelt Library
        511 Albany Post Road
        Hyde Park, NY 12538
        Phone: 914-229-8114

Deadline: Mid-October, mid-March.

Award Amount: Up to $2,500 for travel and related expenses.

Purpose of Grant/Fellowship and Restrictions: The award is meant to support travel to the Library in Hyde Park, New York. Research revolving around Franklin and Eleanor Roosevelt and their associates, especially projects that are likely to be published and are of benefit to educators and policy makers, are most likely to be supported. The Library is also interested in giving grants to citizens of emerging democracies in Third World countries.

H. Harry S Truman Library

Address: Harry S Truman Library
U.S. Highway 24 and Delaware Street
Independence, MO 64050-1798
Phone: 816-833-0425

Deadline: Early January, April, July, and October for research grants; early February for dissertation fellowships.

Award Notification: 6 weeks after deadline for research grants; early April for dissertation fellowships.

Number of Awards: Up to 50 per year for research grants; 2 dissertation fellowships.

Award Amount: Up to $2,500 for research grants; $16,000 for dissertation fellowships.

Purpose of Grant/Fellowship and Restrictions: **Research grants** are intended to support research at the Library for one to three weeks and can include travel, per diem expenses, books, supplies, and copying. Research should revolve around Truman's public career and his presidential administration. **Dissertation Fellowships** are meant to support the writing of the dissertation after research has been concluded.

Application Comments and Advice: Applications for research grants are judged on the amount of material that needs to be researched at the library and the extent to which others have already worked on that material. Be sure to call and confirm that necessary materials are located in the library holdings.

8. Sigma Xi Research Grants[8]

Administrative Agency: Sigma Xi.

Address: Committee on Grants-in-Aid of Research
Sigma Xi Headquarters
99 Alexander Drive—Box 13975
Research Triangle Park, NC 27709
Phone: 800-243-6534

Deadline: February 1, May 1, November 1.

Award Notification: Eight weeks after each closing date.

Award Amount: Up to $1,000, although usual award does not exceed $600. Requests may be made for second-year support for a particular project but not for a third year. Support may be used for travel to a field site, field living expenses, and equipment and supplies not usually found in an institutional research laboratory. *Not funded* are stipends, manuscript preparation, purchase of standard equipment or supplies normally available in an institutional laboratory, or travel to meetings.

Application Form: Most campuses have a faculty member who acts as liaison to Sigma Xi, and he or she should have applications. Applicants should also check the graduate school office or write to the address above.

Purpose of Grant/Fellowship and Restrictions: To support scientific investigation in any field. Grants are available to graduate students at any level as well as to undergraduate students in degree programs.

Applicant Eligibility: Applicants must be enrolled in a degree program.

Application Requirements: A completed application and written statements of support from two faculty members in the field, one of whom is the project advisor.

Application Comments and Advice: This is a short, no-nonsense application. The section allotted to the project description is small; no more than 400 words can be crammed into the area. Applicants are advised to use this space to describe the problem to be solved, where the

8. Based on the 1994 Sigma Xi Application for Grants-in-Aid Research, Sigma Xi.

research is to be done, the plan or methodology for solving the problem, the significance of the research, the application of the results, and how the project fits into a larger research project, if applicable. You may wish to substitute the word "question" for "problem"—the question to be asked, the question to be answered, and so on. The project description must be given a sense of validity and feasibility. Whether the research can be done practically within the time allotted is always a worry to funding agencies.

A second section is allotted to the type of assistance needed and how much it will cost, with a justification for each item.

Further Reading

Annual Register of Grant Support: A Directory of Funding Sources. Ed. R. R. Bowker. Wilmette, IL: National Register Publishing, Macmillan Directory Division. Annual.

Catalog of Federal Domestic Assistance. U.S. General Services Administration. Washington, DC: U.S. Government Printing Office. Annual.

Directory of Grants in the Humanities. Sixth edition. Phoenix, AZ: Oryx Press, 1992.

Directory of Research Grants. Phoenix, AZ: Oryx Press, 1994.

Foundation Grants to Individuals. Ed. Carlotta Mills. New York: Foundation Center, 1993.

Grants, Fellowships, and Prizes of Interest to Historians. Washington, DC: American Historical Association, 1991.

Lefferts, Robert. *Getting a Grant in the 1990s: How to Write Successful Grants Proposals.* Englewood Cliffs, NJ: Prentice-Hall, 1991.

Margolin, Judith, ed. *Foundation Fundamentals: A Guide for Grantseekers.* New York: Foundation Center, 1991.

Morrone, John, ed. *Grants and Awards Available to American Writers.* New York: PEN American Center, 1992.

Smith, Robert. *Graduate Research: A Guide for Students in the Sciences.* New York: Plenum Press, 1990.

Smithsonian Opportunities for Research and Study in History, Art, and Sciences. Washington, DC: Smithsonian Institution. Annual.

Williams, Lisa, ed. *The Grants Register.* Thirteenth edition. New York: St. Martin's Press, 1992.

Chapter 6
Dissertation Fellowships

This chapter provides general information and application writing advice for all the dissertation grants for which a student may apply. It also describes in detail certain specific grant opportunities, namely:

1. American Association of University Women (AAUW) American Fellowships (Dissertation and Postdoctoral)
2. Ford Foundation Dissertation Fellowships for Minorities
3. Guggenheim Dissertation Fellowships
4. Jacob K. Javits Fellowships
5. National Endowment for the Humanities (NEH) Dissertation Grants
6. National Science Foundation (NSF) Grants for Improving Doctoral Dissertation Research
7. Charlotte W. Newcombe Doctoral Dissertation Fellowships
8. Spencer Foundation Dissertation Year Fellowships Related to Education

Persons to Whom These Fellowships Are of Interest: Doctoral students who are researching or writing their dissertations.

Fields Funded by One or More of These Fellowships: Behavioral and social sciences, humanities, sciences, engineering, public health.

Degree Programs Funded by These Fellowships: PhD, DSc, ThD, and other doctoral degrees.

General Information

Dissertation grants may be awarded to support thesis research and/or writing. Some competitions require that ABD (All But Dissertation) status be achieved before application, while others require that the applicant be ABD just prior to receiving the award.

Dissertation funding comes in a variety of types. Some types have been established to support groups of people—like women and minorities—who have not been historically well supported by universities. Fellowships such as the AAUW and the Ford fall into this category. Another type of dissertation award is designed to support students in a specific disciplinary area. The NEH fellowships, for example, are strictly for work done in the humanities. Still a third classification of dissertation support includes those grants that are for specific research. Guggenheim dissertation fellowships, for example, are made available to those who do research on topics of violence, aggression, and dominance. Still other dissertation support is for research abroad. This type is discussed in Chapter 4.

Dissertation funding can provide money for living support, travel, supplies, and equipment. Some fellowships provide small amounts of money, while others can be quite generous.

During the initial stages of dissertation proposal preparation, it is a good idea to start looking for funding. Support can be especially important for students who have outlived their institutional funding and must start relying on external money. In addition, a dissertation fellowship is a good credential and is appealing to hiring institutions, especially in fields where success in winning postdoctoral research funding is expected. A student who wins research or dissertation grants during his or her graduate years is viewed as a person who is more likely to be able to secure money in the future.

It makes sense to reapply for dissertation fellowships if your proposal is rejected the first time around. Not all agencies allow reapplication. Those that do will usually supply reviewers' comments, although you must write to request copies of the remarks. These opinions can be helpful in redirecting the writing of the proposal; sometimes they are basically useless. But until you see them, you cannot know how helpful they will be, so request copies whenever you are considering reapplying.

It is important to figure out whether your project will be of interest to a particular agency. Sometimes you can figure that out by reviewing a list of past winning topics; these are often available from the funding organization upon request. In addition, many of these lists are replicated in the weekly editions of the *Chronicle of Higher Education*, which can be found in most academic offices as well as in the campus library. In some cases it makes sense to call the agency, talk to the fellowship coordinator, and find out if a particular topic is appropriate. NSF is particularly good at guiding students regarding fields and areas of interest. Most organizations are interested in getting the most relevant applications, and so they are usually very helpful to students who call. Certainly if you still have questions after reading the information/ application packet, a phone call can save you a lot of aggravation.

General Application Advice

1. **Begin looking for fellowships when starting to write the dissertation proposal.** The proposal writing stage is a good time to ask faculty and more advanced students what is available in the field. If the institution has an administrator who helps students find funding, visit that person. Since funds are available for the various stages of dissertation work, it is helpful to know early on what is available.

2. **Do not apply for anything until after selecting your dissertation director.** Most agencies rely heavily upon the opinion of the faculty advisor when evaluating proposals. If your dissertation director is not wild with enthusiasm about the project, your likelihood of doing well in a fellowship competition is limited.

3. **Do not just attach the dissertation proposal to every application and hope for the best.** Each funding application is different. Although most agencies want substantially the same information, the order of presentation and amount of space they permit always varies. Be willing to tailor your research project description to the requirements of each individual application opportunity. Fine-tuning takes more time, but the results are worth it.

4. **Do give serious consideration to reapplying if your attempt is rejected.** This is especially true with study abroad fellowships. Also, a year's worth of research always improves focus and usually results in a better application effort.

5. **Know when to borrow money.** For some students, there comes a point when time is better spent finishing the dissertation than sending out more applications. At that point applications for external funding become more time consuming than they are worth. The fellowship-seeking process may interrupt the flow of research or dissertation writing. In the long run it may make better economic sense to finish your degree and concentrate on finding a job or postdoctoral position. This decision is really an individual call and should be made in consultation with your faculty advisor and a financial aid administrator.

Specific Fellowship Opportunities

All information, except the author's advice, is taken from the actual application packets, award announcements, and other documents written by administrative agencies, or on the basis of calls to the individual agencies. Every effort is made to use the same language as that on the application or to paraphrase or summarize that language. For ease of reading, quotation marks are used only to draw special attention to important application sections.

1. American Association of University Women (AAUW) American Fellowships (Dissertation and Postdoctoral)[1]

Administrative Agency: American Association of University Women.

Address: AAUW Educational Foundation
P.O. Box 4030
Iowa City, IA 52243-4030
Phone: 202-728-7617 (program information)
319-337-1716 (for application)

Deadline: Mid-November.

Award Notification: Mid-April.

Number of Awards: Up to 50 per competition for dissertations; 9 for postdocs.

Average Number of Applicants: 950 per competition for dissertations; 200 for postdocs.

Award Amount: $14,500 for dissertations; $20,000–25,000 for postdoctoral awards.

Application Form: Applications are available after August of each year from the address above.

Purpose of Grant/Fellowship and Restrictions: The AAUW was established for the purpose of promoting equity for women through education. To this end the foundation funds a variety of fellowship and grant programs. The American Fellowships were established to support the final

1. Based on the 1994–1995 American Association of University Women American Fellowships, American Association of University Women.

year of dissertation writing in any field. AAUW Selected Professions Fellowships are available for the final year of study in a variety of programs in architecture, computer/information science, engineering, mathematics/statistics, business, law, and medicine. In addition, the program supports postdoctoral research. The description here focuses on the dissertation fellowships. For more information on postdocs and predissertation research contact the AAUW Educational Foundation.

Length of Award: One year.

Applicant Eligibility: Applicants should be women who are finished with all their requirements for a doctoral degree in the sciences, humanities, and social sciences except for the dissertation. The American Fellowships are for the final year of dissertation writing and are not meant for research. Applicants should anticipate completing the doctoral degree around the end of the fellowship year. American Fellowships support living and educational expenses.

Students who have received an external dissertation writing fellowship just prior to when they might use an AAUW American Fellowship are not eligible.

Application Requirements: A completed application consisting of a narrative autobiography, curriculum vitae, five-page project statement, institutional certification form, three letters of recommendation, and official transcripts.

Application Comments and Advice: AAUW is not only interested in enhancing the career potential of women through education but in supporting women who are committed to helping other women. This does not necessarily mean that the dissertation topic must be about women (although that is a plus), but it is certain that a dedication to making the lot of other women better through participation in organizations, research, teaching, advising, or counseling is important. That commitment should be made very clear in the Narrative Autobiography.

The Statement of Project should not be the dissertation proposal. While the instructions leave the content up to the applicant, it makes sense to prepare a statement that includes a summary of your project, your methodology, the significance of your research to the academic and/or non-academic community, the originality of your work, the subsequent impact your work might have on future research in the field, a time table (including work already accomplished and a writing schedule), an assurance that you will complete your doctorate within the required time frame, and a one-page bibliography.

2. Ford Foundation Dissertation Fellowships for Minorities[2]

Administrative Agency: National Research Council.

Address: The Fellowship Office
National Research Council
2101 Constitution Avenue
Washington, DC 20418
Phone: 202-334-2872

Deadline: Early November.

Award Notification: Early April.

Number of Awards: 20 per competition.

Average Number of Applicants: 200 per competition.

Award Amount: $18,000.

Application Form: Applicants should check with the graduate school or minority office or write to the address above.

Purpose of Grant/Fellowship and Restrictions: The Ford Foundation is interested in helping minority students finish PhD or DSc degrees. Fields supported include all research-based programs in the behavioral and social sciences, humanities, engineering, mathematics, physical sciences, and biological sciences and interdisciplinary programs that combine these disciplines. Fields *not* funded include business administration and management, health sciences, public health, home economics, library science, speech pathology and audiology, personnel and guidance, social work, fine arts and performing arts, and education.

Dissertation students should have finished all their degree requirements except the dissertation. The fellowship is for the final year, and applicants should be able to finish the degree within the funding year.

Length of Award: One year.

Applicant Eligibility: Applicants should be U.S. citizens or U.S. na-

---

2. Based on the 1993–1994 Ford Foundation Predoctoral and Dissertation Fellowships for Minorities, National Research Council.

tionals and enrolled in a U.S. non-profit institution of higher education. Ethnicity is restricted to the following groups: Alaskan Natives, Native American Indians, Black/African Americans, Mexican Americans/Chicanos, Native Pacific Islanders, and Puerto Ricans.

Application Requirements: A two-part application that includes verification of doctoral degree status form, dissertation abstract, plan for completion of degree, official transcripts, and two references (one from the dissertation adviser). A resume, two additional references, and dissertation bibliography may also be sent if desired.

Application Comments and Advice: The dissertation abstract should include a description of the problem and the research methodology. The significance of the research should be emphasized in the abstract and again in the Proposed Plan for Completion of the Doctoral Degree. The more original and significant a project is, the more likely an award.

3. Guggenheim Dissertation Fellowships[3]

Administrative Agency: The Harry Frank Guggenheim Foundation.

Address: Harry Frank Guggenheim Foundation
527 Madison Avenue
New York, NY 10022-4304
Phone: 212-644-4907

Deadline: Early February.

Award Notification: June.

Number of Awards: 10 per competition.

Average Number of Applicants: 150 per competition.

Award Amount: $10,000.

Application Form: Applicants should check with the graduate school office or write to the address above.

---

3. Based on the 1994–1995 Harry Frank Guggenheim Foundation Dissertation Fellowship, Harry Frank Guggenheim Foundation.

Purpose of Grant/Fellowship and Restrictions: The fellowship was established several years ago to support only the writing year of dissertation work. The Foundation is aware that in some disciplines research and writing can take place within the same year and accepts that premise when presented cogently. Nonetheless, applicants are expected to finish their dissertations within the 12-month funding period.

The objective of the fellowship is to fund research dealing with violence, aggression, and dominance. While they are interested in human behavior in these areas, the Foundation is also interested in behavior that is found in other species as well. Projects from the social and natural sciences are of interest.

Dissertations that contribute to the understanding and amelioration of violence, aggression, and dominance are of most interest. The Foundation is especially tuned to topics that apply to social change, the socialization of children, intergroup conflict, drug trafficking and use, family relationships, and investigations of control, aggression, and violence.

Length of Award: Twelve months.

Applicant Eligibility: The fellowship must be used for the dissertation writing year.

Application Requirements: An application that includes two letters of reference, a research plan of around 15 double-spaced typed pages, assurances of human or animal subject right protection, applicant and advisor's curriculum vitae, and official transcripts. Applicants should send 6 copies of everything.

The Foundation lists the biggest mistakes made by applicants as the following: applications made prematurely (that is, the applicant cannot possibly finish during the support period); projects that are not relevant to violence, aggression, and dominance; applications where only one copy is sent or where all copies are sent uncollated; applications where the advisor's letter and/or c.v. arrive separately and/or late and/or where just one copy is sent; and applications that do not include a research plan.

Application Comments and Advice: It is clear that the rules must be read carefully and scrupulously followed. Failure to comply with the smallest requirement seems to ensure that the application will not be considered. Some agencies are flexible, but this one is not.

This application is time-consuming and should only be undertaken when the subject area is a perfect fit. If the fit is cloudy, then call the Foundation.

The research plan is the key element. Although 10 to 15 pages is said to be a typical length, proposals may be longer or shorter. The dissertation proposal may be the basis for the plan, but information about what has been accomplished since the proposal and a detailed plan for completion should also be included. Relevance to the Foundation's interest should be clearly delineated in the research plan even though a statement to that effect is asked for elsewhere on the application. You must also make clear in the research plan that the dissertation will be completed within the funding time frame. Relevance to violence, aggression, and dominance as well as the prospects for completing within the time frame should be reemphasized in the letter from the dissertation advisor.

4. Jacob K. Javits Fellowships[4]

The basics of this fellowship are described in Chapter 3. In the spring of 1994 the Javits Board eliminated the dissertation support component, and currently limits application to students who have no more than thirty graduate credits at the time of application. We have chosen nevertheless to include the fellowship as it has most recently been described. Students whose dissertation areas seem to fit the requirements may wish to contact the fellowship office to determine its current status.

Administrative Agency: U.S. Department of Education.

Address: Jacob K. Javits Fellowships
P.O. Box 84
Washington, DC 20044
Phone: 800-4-FED-AID; 202-708-9415

Deadline: ———

Award Notification: ———

Application Comments and Advice: The fellowship has in the past been available to support dissertation research in the humanities, social

---

4. Based on the 1994–1995 Jacob J. Javits Fellowships, U.S. Department of Education.

sciences, and fine arts. Projects of local or regional significance were not as intriguing as those with national import, which were in turn not as appealing as those that might be considered of significance to a world audience.

5. National Endowment for the Humanities (NEH) Dissertation Grants[5]

Administrative Agency: National Endowment for the Humanities.

Address: NEH
Dissertation Grants Program
1100 Pennsylvania Avenue NW, Room 316
Washington, DC 20506
Phone: 202-606-8438

Deadline: Mid-November.

Award Notification: Late May.

Number of Awards: 25 to 50 per competition, depending upon money available.

Average Number of Applicants: 1,400 per competition (see below under Special Application Information).

Award Amount: $14,000.

Application Form: Applicants should check with the graduate school or humanities division office. Students must apply through the institution; they cannot apply directly to the Endowment (see Special Application Information below).

Purpose of Grant/Fellowship and Restrictions: The grant supports one full year of doctoral dissertation writing in history; philosophy; languages; linguistics; literature; archaeology; jurisprudence; the history, theory, and criticism of the arts; ethics; comparative religion; any social science that uses historical or philosophical approaches; and other fields that can be construed as belonging in the humanities. The Endowment also establishes special interest topics every year that are found in the

5. Based on the 1994–1995 National Endowment for the Humanities Dissertation Grants, National Endowment for the Humanities.

application packet. Past topics have included the Columbian Quincentenary and the Emergence of Democracy.

Length of Award: One year.

Applicant Eligibility: Applicants must be U.S. citizens or U.S. Samoan nationals enrolled in a U.S. institution in a humanities field. They should have ABD status, have an approved dissertation topic, and be able to complete the dissertation within the grant year.

Application Requirements: A completed application, which includes a confirmation of nomination and eligibility form, a resume, two letters of reference (one from the dissertation advisor), a list of graduate courses taken, a description of the dissertation project, and a bibliography. Applicants should send 9 collated copies of the application.

During the first competition in 1992–1993 students applied directly to the Endowment. The response was overwhelming in numbers. Subsequently, a rule was instituted requiring students to be nominated through a campus office.

No more than two grants may be awarded to students at a single institution in each application year. No more than 10 students may be nominated by a single university in each application year. Each university has a designated nominating official, who is probably located in the humanities division or graduate school. Applicants should contact the nominating official at their institution for on-campus deadlines and local nomination procedures.

Application Comments and Advice: The application information makes it clear that the support is skewed toward dissertation writing rather than research. A six page double-spaced project description requests a narrative explaining the dissertation conception, definition, organization, plan of completion, chapter outline, and summary of work done prior to the application. A separate page may be used for bibliographic information.

Clearly the most important aspect of this application once the project description is done is the significance of the dissertation topic to scholars in the field and its contribution in the way of new knowledge to the discipline. The more significant the dissertation, the more likely it is to be supported. This point should be stressed to referees. In addition, the Endowment is concerned about a student's dedication to research and teaching, which should be clearly delineated in the Statement of Professional Goals.

6. National Science Foundation (NSF) Grants for Improving Doctoral Dissertation Research[6]

Administrative Agency: The National Science Foundation.

Address: National Science Foundation
Forms and Publication Unit
4201 Wilson Boulevard
Arlington, VA 22230
Phone: 703-306-1130 (for application)
Phone: 703-306-1760 (Directorate of Social, Behavioral, and Economic Sciences)
Phone: 703-306-1483 (Directorate of Environmental Biology)

Deadline: Usually six months before funding is needed. Applicants should check with specific program but program should be called.

Number of Awards: Up to 200 per year for all programs in social, behavioral, and economic studies; up to 75 in the biological sciences.

Average Number of Applicants: 25–33 percent of applications per year for social, behavioral, and economic directorate (percentage differs for programs within the directorate); 30 percent of applications per year for the biological sciences.

Award Amount: Up to $12,000 in the social, behavioral, and economic sciences; average award in biology of $10,000–12,000.

Application Form: Applicants should inquire in the on-campus research office for a copy of *Grants for Research and Education in Science and Engineering* (GRESE, NSF 92-89), or the most current version of this application booklet, or they should write to the address above.

Purpose of Grant/Fellowship and Restrictions: Dissertation improvement grants are available through some but not all programs sponsored by NSF. Research is supported through the Directorate of Social, Behavioral, and Economic Sciences to support dissertation research most actively in anthropology; decision, risk, and management science; geography and regional science; linguistics; law and social sci-

6. Based on the 1992 Grants for Research and Education in Science and Engineering, National Sciences Foundation.

ences; political science; sociology; and studies in science, technology, and society (including ethics and value studies). Grants are also available through the Directorate of Environmental Biology for research in ecology studies; systematic biology; population biology; animal behavior; and functional and physiologic ecology. Support is not available for primarily human or animal disease-related research.

Support through the Directorate of Social, Behavioral, and Economic Sciences is primarily to fund data collection and field research not routinely supported by the home university. Expenses such as survey costs, microfilms, payments to subjects, special research equipment, data analysis, travel, and field living expenses may be covered. Stipends (other than field living expenses), tuition, and fees are not covered.

A description of support made through the Directorate of Environmental Biology is available by calling NSF.

In all programs, application must be made through the university in which the applicant is enrolled with the dissertation advisor and applicant as co-principal investigators.

Students who are interested in this grant should call the number above and ask for the telephone number of the specific program that supports research in their field. The program (such as anthropology or animal behavior, for example) should be contacted for specific information about how interested the program is in the specific project, how much money is available for projects, and the recommended application procedure. *No application should be made without a preliminary phone call to the proper program.*

Length of Award: Depends upon project.

Applicant Eligibility: Students must be enrolled in a doctoral dissertation program in the fields mentioned above.

Application Requirements: A GRESE, NSF 92-89 form plus instructions from the specific program. For the Directorate of Social, Behavioral, and Economic Sciences the basic application includes: a 200-word project summary; a project description of no longer than 10 single-spaced, typed pages; a detailed budget; a research schedule; a description of current support; a short curriculum vitae for the applicant and the dissertation advisor; human or animal subjects study approval, if required; copies of surveys or questionnaires, if applicable; and anything else the specific program may require.

Application Comments and Advice: As stated above, nothing should be done until after you have phoned the specific program to see how enthusiastic they are about your project and what local, programmatic rules have been established for application. Clearly, your dissertation advisor must complete endorse the project and be willing to serve as CO-PI.

7. Charlotte W. Newcombe Doctoral Dissertation Fellowships[7]

Administrative Agency: The Woodrow Wilson National Fellowship Foundation.

Address: Woodrow Wilson Foundation
CN 5281
Princeton, NJ 08543-5281
Phone: 609-924-4666

Deadline: Mid-November for application requests; mid-December for application submission from within the United States or Canada; late November for application submission from outside the United States or Canada.

Award Notification: April.

Number of Awards: Up to 40 per competition.

Average Number of Applicants: 500 per competition.

Award Amount: $12,500 to be used over 12 months. An allowance for medical insurance.

Application Form: Applicants should write to the address above.

Purpose of Grant/Fellowship and Restrictions: The organization supports research in the area of ethical or religious values in the humanities and social sciences. Areas of interest include the ethical implications of foreign policy, values that influence political decisions, moral codes of cultures, and religious and ethical issues reflected in history or litera-

---

7. Based on the 1994–1995 Charlotte W. Newcombe Doctoral Dissertation Fellowships, Woodrow Wilson National Foundation.

ture. Issues of the broadest significance and those that help bring an understanding of how religion and ethics give substance to people's lives are of the most interest.

The fellowship supports dissertation writing. It is expected that awardees will complete their degrees shortly after the funding year.

Length of Award: One year.

Applicant Eligibility: Applicants must have completed all of their doctoral work except the dissertation at a U.S. university.

Application Requirements: A completed application includes official transcripts, three letters of reference, and a dissertation prospectus of six pages or less. Reapplications are not accepted.

Students who win the award may not have funding from other sources that duplicate this fellowship. Recipients may not work for pay for more than 6–8 hours a week while they are receiving Newcombe Fellowship funds.

Application Comments and Advice: Careful attention should be given to explaining the dissertation's relevance to the funding agency's research interests in ethical or religious values in the humanities. The significance of the dissertation to the field and the contribution of new knowledge within the framework of ethical or religious values is critical.

8. Spencer Foundation Dissertation Year Fellowships Related to Education[8]

Administrative Agency: The Spencer Foundation.

Address: The Spencer Foundation
900 North Michigan Avenue
Suite 2800
Chicago, IL 60611
Phone: 312-337-7000

Deadline: Mid-October for application requests; early November for completed applications.

---

8. Based on the 1994–1994 Spencer Foundation Dissertation Fellowships for Research Related to Education, Spencer Foundation.

Award Notification: April.

Number of Awards: 30 per competition.

Average Number of Applicants: Information not available.

Award Amount: $15,000, which can be used over 2 years.

Application Form: Applicants should write to the address above.

Purpose of Grant/Fellowship and Restrictions: The Foundation wishes to support research that "can improve education around the world." The fellowship is meant for doctoral students in a variety of disciplines, including anthropology, architecture, art history, economics, education, history, linguistics, literature, philosophy, political science, public health, psychology, religion, sociology, and other fields as well. Recent topics have included pedagogy and political culture in the Soviet Union in the 1930s, Dewey's philosophy of education, and Native American culture and education. The history, theory, and practice of education worldwide are of interest to the Foundation.

Length of Award: Up to two years.

Applicant Eligibility: Applicants must be enrolled in a doctoral program at a U.S. institution and must be ABD. The fellowship is for support of the data analysis and writing stages of the dissertation process.

Application Requirements: A completed application, which consists of transcripts, 2 letters of reference, a personal statement, the dissertation abstract, and a plan for dissertation completion not longer than eight double-spaced pages.

Application Comments and Advice: Three components, which should be seen as three parts to a whole, are important to the application. The first is a dissertation abstract, the second is a narrative discussion of the dissertation of no more than seven double-spaced pages, and the third is a plan for completing the project of no more than one page. The dissertation abstract should delineate the nature of your research with emphasis on the significance and originality of the work and its relevance to and impact on education. The narrative discussion should flesh out the abstract by adding substance, especially to the importance of the work to the field. Give special attention to discussing any innovative findings that facilitate improving the understanding of the history, theory, and practice of education.

The Foundation makes it clear that funding is for support of the writing year (although they recognize that time and financial constraints may mean two years of part-time writing). The Work Plan should include a discussion of what work you have already done as well as a strategy for completing the dissertation and the degree. The Work Plan should be carefully conceived because it becomes, in the event of an award, a financial disbursement arrangement.

Further Reading

Krathwohl, David. *How to Prepare a Research Proposal: Guidelines for Funding and Dissertations in the Social Sciences*. Syracuse, NY: Syracuse University Press, 1988.

Locke, Lawrence F., Waneen Wyrick Spirduso, and Stephen J. Silverman. *Proposals That Work: A Guide for Planning Dissertations and Grant Proposals*. Newbury Park, CA: Sage Publications, 1993.

Rudestam, Kjell Erik and Rae R. Newton. *Surviving Your Dissertation: A Comprehensive Guide to Content and Process*. Newbury Park, CA: Sage Publications, 1992.

Sternberg, David. *How to Complete and Survive a Doctoral Dissertation*. New York: St. Martin's Press, 1981.

Chapter 7
Postdoctoral Fellowships

Mary Morris Heiberger and Julia Miller Vick

A postdoctoral research opportunity, often known as a "postdoc," is a short-term appointment, frequently for one or two years, usually, although not always, done immediately on the completion of a doctorate. The rate of compensation typically falls between the level of a graduate student stipend and an assistant professor's salary. Science postdoctoral appointments often are for at least two years. Year-long opportunities are most commonly found in the social sciences and humanities.

In the sciences, postdoctoral experience has long been the norm for anyone planning a research-based career. It has been less common in the social sciences, and unusual in the humanities. However, in the past several years the percentages of new PhDs in all fields accepting postdoctoral research opportunities has increased, with the greatest rate of growth in the humanities, as shown in Table 3.

Postdoctoral opportunities fall into two broad categories. Some are endowed, ongoing positions that a candidate must identify and apply for through a formal, often highly competitive process. Many of these are available through large government agencies, foundations, or research centers at universities, and they can be identified through standard directory resources. Particularly in the social sciences and humanities, they require the candidate to propose a research project, and funding is awarded in terms of that specific research proposal. Of these institutionalized opportunities, some are "portable," meaning that the funding can be taken anywhere, while others require resident research at a particular institution.

Other positions are more ad hoc and temporary. They are created by a researcher's grant money and support work on a project already proposed and funded by the senior researcher. These opportunities

TABLE 3. Percentage of New PhDs Accepting Postdoctoral Positions

Year	All fields	Social sciences	Humanities	Life sciences	Physical sciences
1971	15.8	7.6	2.5	39.7	35.5
1981	19.3	13.6	4.2	53.6	34.2
1991	27.5	17.4	7.3	62.4	48.5

Source: Taken from the *Summary Report, 1991: Doctorate Recipients from United States Universities* (Washington, DC: National Academy Press, 1993), Table 10, p. 21.

are identified by seeking out, not so much institutions, as individuals doing specific research. Hiring, while it may be highly competitive in terms of selectivity, can be as informal a procedure as a phone call to a researcher followed by a letter, a c.v., and a highly enthusiastic recommendation from your advisor. By definition, all these latter postdocs require work in the senior researcher's location.

This chapter will discuss the reasons for doing a postdoc, as well as some of the pitfalls of doing one for too long; address some specific considerations and opportunities in the sciences and in the social sciences and humanities; suggest ways to identify and apply for positions; give some consideration for evaluating openings; and list representative postdocs.

General Information

There are many reasons for doing postdoctoral work. Such positions can help new PhDs branch out from the narrowly defined specialty created by their dissertation work. By broadening your area of expertise, you may become a more desirable candidate when going on the job market seeking a tenure-track position. If you are perceived as "stuck" in a very narrowly defined specialty, a hiring department may have little interest. If you are a bit more "rounded out," you may be seen as a person who can fill both research and teaching gaps in the department.

If you are one of those unfortunate people who learned too late that someone was doing basically the same dissertation that you were, a postdoc can offer you the chance to redefine your research so that it is different from that of other scholars.

If the job market is terrible, doing a postdoc "buys time" for further research or enhancement of teaching skills. Although the researcher is not in a tenure-track position, he or she has the opportunity to think about the future course of scholarship, develop new mentoring relationships, get to know more people in the field, and apply for more jobs. Furthermore, since tenure decisions are often heavily based on a candidate's research record, the research done during a postdoc, often without teaching obligations, can help enhance the total amount of research production you need when it comes time to be evaluated for tenure.

In science, postdocs are usually a prerequisite for research-oriented academic positions. Most research-intensive universities and many small colleges will not even consider a candidate for assistant or associate professor positions without a couple of years of postdoctoral experience. In businesses such as the pharmaceutical industry, postdocs are also virtually required for research positions.

In the social sciences and humanities, postdocs are often done in order to wait out a poor job market or to build a stronger research record. However, PhD students are now more frequently looking at postdocs as opportunities to enhance their research abilities and deepen their research area before hunting for a tenure-track position.

General Application Advice

Begin early, at least 24 months before you are due to finish your degree. It will take time to identify and research openings and submit applications. Some positions will have application deadlines close to a year in advance of the starting time. Therefore, even if a postdoc is your second choice, it is important to plan to pursue it simultaneously with the academic job search.

Use all means possible to identify opportunities. The most important place to begin the exploration is with your dissertation advisor. If you are in the sciences, where postdocs tend to be *de rigueur* for research careers, your advisor may regularly refer graduates to good postdoctoral positions in colleagues' labs. As will be discussed later, this can be a mixed blessing, especially if your research interests are beginning to diverge from that of your advisor. In any case, an advisor's contacts, recommendations, and support will be of the utmost importance, so what he or she says must be taken seriously. Advisors and other faculty members in the department will often be aware of additional programs and opportunities for which past students have successfully competed.

The next step is to move on to using all print and computer resources mentioned in Chapter 2. Inquire everywhere. In many fields, for example, scholars who participate in electronic lists on the Internet will respond to each other's inquiries as to what organizations may be interested in funding a particular type of research.

In addition to staying alert for formally announced postdocs, make inquiries with researchers with whom you wish to work or with institutions with which it is desirable to be affiliated. In the sciences, where externally funded research is the norm, identify the researchers whose work is exciting, learn as much as possible about their work through their publications (resources in the library make this a straightforward task), and then contact them directly to express interest.

In some cases, it may be preferable to have faculty members who are familiar with your research make an advance phone call on your behalf. It is completely appropriate, however, to send a copy of a curriculum vitae, with a letter expressing interest, directly to the researcher, and then to follow up with a phone call. If you easily establish rapport with people by phone, it may be better to call first to explore the availability of positions and then follow up with a letter, c.v., and possible reprints of publications. If you actively attend professional meetings, as should be the case, face-to-face meetings with potential postdoc supervisors may be arranged. At the University of Pennsylvania, where our survey of new PhDs asks how they obtained their positions, a frequent answer is, "I contacted researchers whose work interested me."

The same approach to a researcher that is effective in the sciences is also appropriate in the social sciences and humanities, where there are fewer large sponsored research grants. In some cases, however, it may be more effective to approach a researcher more as a point of contact with her or his institution rather than as a direct source of funding. Perhaps in response to the availability of candidates in recent years, more universities are creating postdoctoral positions in the social sciences and humanities. In some cases, especially in large private institutions with high undergraduate tuition, the establishment of these opportunities has come about as a response to undergraduate parent demands for small classes taught by faculty with doctoral degrees. Large classes in the humanities and social sciences and great numbers of courses taught by teaching assistants without their degrees have been roundly criticized by both undergraduates and their parents and have come under close scrutiny by universities. A lower-cost alternative to hiring more full-time, tenure-track faculty is to hire more postdocs with teaching and research responsibilities.

If you seek an opportunity to be at the same institution as a senior researcher whose work you admire, contact that individual, whether or not he or she has access to external funding, to explore ways to become affiliated with his or her institution. This approach may merely lead to a one- or two-year teaching appointment, which would not be precisely the postdoctoral research post you were seeking, but it could lead to the creation of an institutional postdoc of which you might be the recipient. Even though you succeed in identifying opportunities informally, you will still have to make a formal application. At a minimum, you will always need to submit a curriculum vitae, letters of recommendation, and some form of written discussion of research and perhaps teaching interest.

A curriculum vitae, vita, or "c.v." (the terms are interchangeable) is the document that summarizes your qualifications. The construction of a curriculum vitae is beyond the scope of this chapter. However, we do stress that your version must be clear, error-free, and visually appealing. It should be constructed in such a way that the material of most probable interest to the person or committee who will be reading it is the most visually prominent part of the document. Do not content yourself with looking at a fellow student's and modeling yours after it. Consult professional sources, such as those produced by scholarly associations, as well as other materials on curriculum vitae construction. The *Academic Job Search Handbook* (Philadelphia: University of Pennsylvania Press, 1992) gives an extensive discussion about vita preparation and provides examples from many disciplines.

Recommendations have already been discussed, so there is little to add here. However, if a proposal to do a specific piece of research is being submitted, it will be important to ask recommenders to discuss the significance and promise of the research itself in addition to your strengths as a candidate.

For some applications, such as those with a single supervisor, the written discussion may merely take the form of a cover letter succinctly stating the research interest that coincides with the supervisor's and possible contributions you could make to his or her lab, including knowledge of particular techniques or the ability to develop equipment. If a full-scale research proposal is required, all these ideas will have to be fleshed out in greater detail. Everything that has been discussed in terms of applying for dissertation support (see Chapter 6) is relevant to writing a proposal for postdoctoral support.

The standards for obtaining academic positions now are even higher than in the past. By completing the PhD, you have received the calling card into the international community of scholars. Particularly in the social sciences and humanities, the graduate is no longer an apprentice but is instead expected to contribute to the universal body of new knowledge. A postdoc in these areas is far less likely to be funded to do something that will primarily strengthen the candidate's own skill and knowledge base. When writing a proposal for a postdoc in the social sciences and humanities, it is very important to be clear about how the short-term proposal fits into longer-term academic goals. How much can realistically be expected to be accomplished during the postdoctoral period, and in some cases how additional funding resources would be pursued, may need to be included.

With such limited monies available, funding agencies would prefer to think they are making a long-term investment in scholarship that is very significant and in scholars who will be very productive for some time to come.

Naturally you need to evaluate the whole process of pursuing postdoctoral research positions carefully. Why waste time preparing an application for something you do not want anyway? Nevertheless, it is wise to apply broadly enough to be sure of obtaining something, and you may well end up with more than one opening to consider.

While thinking about opportunities, give serious thought to personal considerations such as salary, geographic location, and family needs. In professional terms, there are also several things everyone should consider. Probably the most important consideration is with whom to work. While this question weighs in most heavily when you are seeking a position working on another researcher's grant, it is crucial even when being funded to do individual scholarship. The colleagues with whom you surround yourself will most likely have a profound impact on the research outcomes. On a personal level, they can help make a typical workday anything from pleasantly challenging to a terrible nightmare. Colleagues may also serve as important sources of recommendations and leads for pursuing permanent positions, funding opportunities, or publication advice. So be sure to consider the quality of their work, their reputations in the field, and whatever personal characteristics they bring to the workplace.

When choosing a supervisor (which is as important as the supervisor's choosing you), consider the person's track record in working with and supporting postdocs. A good way to do this is to speak directly with some of the researcher's current or most recent postdoctoral associates. To some extent this can be done by consulting standard library sources and examining the supervisor's publications and the publications of postdocs who have worked directly for him or her. In addition, talking directly to the supervisor about the career paths of recent postdocs is helpful. It is also important to find out, through informal conversation with people who have been postdocs or who are at the same institution, what the supervisor is like to work with. This latter process is useful not only in deciding whether to accept a position but also in getting to know the supervisor's style and in ultimately getting the postdoc off to a good start if you accept it.

An additional consideration for foreign nationals may be whether the postdoc supervisor is someone who will act as a sponsor for U.S. permanent residency if you want that status. Having a "green card" is a tremendous advantage when going on the job market in the United States. Offers that may include this option should be given particular attention.

Specific Postdoctoral Opportunities in the Sciences and Engineering

Scientific postdocs are especially likely to be funded by a senior researcher's grant and to have been chosen on account of her or his field of expertise, rather than institutional affiliation. A very common mechanism for linking candidates and positions is by word of mouth, where an advisor calls a peer on behalf of a student and strongly recommends the individual for a position. This system has certain advantages and disadvantages for candidates.

If you are lucky enough to have a very good relationship with an advisor who has a network of colleagues of national or international stature, and you are interested in continuing in the research direction of the advisor and/or the people to whom he or she can recommend you, this personal referral system makes the process of finding a postdoc a fairly easy one on your part. The only negative aspect of this system is that the skills you need in order to "hustle" for a position will have to be learned later.

In a variation of this system, a student sometimes simply continues with his or her current advisor as a postdoc after completing the doctoral degree. This is an attractive option if you are midway through an important research project that is likely to continue to yield substantial results or if the advisor is about to undertake an exiting new project that appeals to you and with which it is important to be affiliated.

If, however, continued work with your advisor is not desirable, if the advisor does not make recommendations to close associates, or if you are attracted by a shift in research interest, it makes sense not to limit yourself to the contacts provided by the advisor. In many cases, students prefer to search more proactively on their own, as described above. It is very important, however, to secure your advisor's blessing for all postgraduation activities. Nothing can be more harmful to a student's career than a disgruntled dissertation supervisor's negative comments.

Postdocs in industry are another option sought by students, most commonly in chemical and pharmaceutical companies. While these can provide valuable industry experience, you must generally keep in mind that they are still postdoctoral experiences and not career-track research and development positions. Do *not* assume that an industrial postdoc represents a "foot in the door" at the company, unless you have received articulated evidence that that is in fact the case. Commonly, companies make a practice of not hiring their own postdocs. Therefore, it may not be wise to accept a postdoc at an organization that is your first choice for subsequent permanent employment.

Most funding for scientific postdocs comes from the U.S. government. The two primary sources are the National Science Foundation (primarily, although not exclusively, for the physical sciences) and the National Institutes of Health (for the biomedical sciences). Other agencies such as the Departments of Agriculture, Defense, and Energy and NASA also offer postdocs.

Direct funding from the federal government to the individual usually requires U.S. citizenship or permanent resident status. Foreign nationals who are not permanent residents may be funded as postdocs on another individual's federal research grant if funding is channeled through the researcher's institution.

1. National Science Foundation Postdoctoral Programs[1]

NSF is a major source of science postdoctoral funding that sponsors twelve postdoctoral fellowship programs. Information about programs can be gotten from the NSF offices located in Arlington, Virginia. For more general information contact:

Administrative Agency: The National Science Foundation.

Address: The National Science Foundation
4201 Wilson Blvd.
Arlington, VA 22230
E-Mail: stis-request@nsf.gov (Internet); stis-req@NSF (Bitnet)
Phone: 703-306-1234
TDD: 703-306-0090

Administrative offices and phone numbers for individual programs are listed below.

A. BIO Minority Postdoctoral Research Fellowship

1. Based on the National Science Foundation Postdoctoral Programs, National Science Foundation.

Administrative Office: BIO Minority Research Fellowship Program.

Phone: 703-306-1469

B. *Fellowship Opportunities in Environmental Biology for PhDs*

Administrative Office: Division of Environmental Biology.

Phone: 703-306-1480

C. *Postdoctoral Research Fellowships in Plant Biology*

Administrative Office: Division of Biological Instrumentation and Resources.

Phone: 703-306-1422

D. *Earth Sciences Postdoctoral Research Fellowship*

Administrative Office: Division of Earth Sciences.

Phone: 703-306-1557

E. *Minority Postdoctoral Research Fellowship*

Administrative Office: Division of Social, Behavioral, and Economic Research

Phone: 703-306-1733

F. *Japan Society for the Promotion of Science (JSPS) Postdoctoral Awards for U.S. Researchers*

Administrative Office: Division of International Programs.

Phone: 703-306-1701

G. *Science and Technology Agency of Japan Postdoctoral Awards for U.S. Researchers*

Administrative Office: Division of International Programs.

Phone: 703-306-1701

H. *Mathematical Sciences Postdoctoral Research Fellowships*
   (with Research Instructorship Option)

Administrative Office: Division of Mathematical Sciences.

Phone: 703-306-1870

I. *Postdoctoral Research Fellowships in Chemistry*

Administrative Office: Division of Chemistry.

Phone: 703-306-1840

J. *NSF-NATO Postdoctoral Fellowships in Science and Engineering*

Administrative Office: Division of Graduate Education and Research
Development.

Phone: 703-306-1696

K. *Long- and Medium-Term Research Visits for Scientists and Engineers*
   at Foreign Centers of Excellence

Administrative Office: Division of International Programs.

Phone: 703-306-1706

2. National Institutes of Health Individual Research Service Awards[2]

NIH offers approximately 1,600 Individual Research Service Awards each year at the postdoctoral level. Before submitting an application, a candidate must arrange for appointment to an appropriate institution and demonstrate acceptance by a sponsor who will supervise the training and research experience. The institutional setting may be private or public and may include a federal laboratory. The sponsor must document, in the application, the research training plan and the availability of staff and facilities to provide a suitable environment for performing high-quality work. Your sponsor should be a competent, active investigator who works in the area of the proposed research activity and who will personally supervise your progress.

Application packets and explanatory materials, including advice on writing successful applications, are available from:

Address: National Institutes of Health
Office of Grants Inquiries
Division of Research Grants
Bethesda, MD 20892
Phone: 301-594-7248 (includes voice mail ordering options)

NIH information is also available electronically on the Grant Line. The principal documents are the weekly issues of the NIH *Guide for Grants and Contracts*, the official organ for announcing grant information.

The accessing procedure is as follows:

1. Dial 1-301-402-2221. The baud rate is 2400, settings for terminal emulator are even, parity, 7 data bits, 1 stop bit, half duplex.
2. At the connect signal, type gen 1.
3. At the prompt for initials, type bb5
4. At the prompt for account number, type ccs2

Contact Dr. John C. James, the Grant Line moderator, by using jqj@nihcu (Bitnet) or jqj@cu.nih.gov (Internet) or call 301-594-7270 if you need help.

---

2. Based on the National Institutes of Health Postdoctoral Programs, National Institutes of Health.

3. Global Change Distinguished Postdoctoral Fellowships and the
   Alexander Hollaender Distinguished Postdoctoral Fellowships[3]

Administrative Agency: Oak Ridge Institute for Science and Education.

Address: Science/Engineering Education Division
Oak Ridge Institute for Science and Education
P.O. Box 117
Oak Ridge, TN 37831-0117
Phone: 615-576-9934

There are also a number of sources of private external funding
support for which students in the sciences may apply directly. Some
examples are listed below; application forms may be obtained through
the administrative agency. Use this list only as a starting point, taking
care to consult the resources discussed above and in the Further Reading section at the end of this chapter.

4. Congressional Fellowships[4]

Administrative Agency: American Association for the Advancement of
Science.

Address: Congressional Fellowships in Science
American Association for the Advancement of Science
Directorate for Science and Policy Programs/Fellowship
   Programs
1333 H Street NW
Washington, DC 20005
Phone: 202-326-6600

Application Comments and Advice: There are about forty of these fellowships administered by the American Association for the Advancement
of Science on behalf of the numerous scientific societies.

5. Helen Hay Whitney Fellowships in the Medical Sciences[5]

Administrative Agency: The Helen Hay Whitney Foundation.

3. Based on the Oak Ridge Associated Universities Postdoctoral Programs, Oak
Ridge Institute for Science and Education.
4. Based on the Congressional Fellowships in Science, American Association for the
Advancement of Science.
5. Based on the Helen Hay Whitney Postdoctoral Fellowships in the Medical Sciences, Helen Hay Whitney Foundation.

Address: The Whitney Foundation
450 East 63rd Street
New York, NY 10021
Phone: 212-751 8228

Deadline: Mid-August.

Award Notification: January.

Number of Awards: Up to 20 per competition.

Average Number of Applicants: 300 per competition.

Award Amount: $25,000 per year.

Purpose of Grant/Fellowship and Restrictions: The goal of the foundation is to increase the number of imaginative, well-trained, and dedicated medical scientists. The fellowships are for early postdoctoral training in all the basic biomedical sciences.

Length of Award: Two or three years.

Applicant Eligibility: Candidates must hold an MD, PhD, or equivalent degree and be in the early stages of their career. Candidates with no prior postdoctoral training are most competitive for these fellowships. Applications from established scientists or advanced fellows will not be considered.

Application Requirements: Applications are available in mid-March. After an initial screening, some candidates are chosen for personal interviews.

6. Jane Coffin Childs Memorial Fund for Medical Research in Cancer[6]

Administrative Agency: Jane Coffin Childs Fund.

Address: Jane Coffin Childs Fund for Medical Research
333 Cedar Street

6. Based on the Jane Coffin Childs Postdoctoral Fellowships for Medical Research, Jane Coffin Childs Fund.

New Haven, CT 06510
Phone: 203-785-4612

Deadline: Early February.

Award Notification: Spring.

Number of Awards: 25 per competition.

Average Number of Applicants: 250 per competition.

Award Amount: $24,000 the first year; $25,000 the second year; $26,000 the third year, with an additional allowance of $750 for each dependent child. An allowance of $1,500 a year toward the cost of research is usually given to the sponsoring research lab, and a travel award will be made to the fellow.

Purpose of Grant/Fellowship and Restrictions: The fellowships are meant to support research in the medical and related sciences on the causes, origins, and treatment of cancer.

Length of Award: Three years.

Applicant Eligibility: Applicants should not have more than one year of postdoctoral experience. They must hold either the MD or PhD degree in the field in which they propose to study, or they must furnish evidence of equivalent training and experience.

Application Requirements: The applicant must supply the names and addresses of three references, one of whom should be the principal predoctoral advisor, a documented outline of the research problem proposed, and the written consent of the laboratory chief and fiscal officer of the host institution.

Specific Postdoctoral Opportunities in the Social Sciences and Humanities

Because few researchers in most disciplines in the social sciences and humanities receive enough money to support postdoctoral fellows, you are most likely to obtain funding by applying directly to external funding agencies or by tapping regular university funds. An occasional exception, as we discussed above, is the chance to work with some very senior faculty. Since more postdocs are beginning to be created in these fields, however, it is important to keep current with the latest information. This can be done by following announcements in the *Chronicle of Higher Education*, *Black Issues in Higher Education*, all the scholarly job listings published through associations and journals, and other publications that focus on grant and fellowship opportunities, such as the periodic funding newsletters *ARIS* and the *Grant Advisor*. In addition, you should talk to people in your department or at meetings about possible openings.

Do not overlook the tremendous amount of information-sharing that occurs via electronic networks. If your campus affords access to worldwide electronic information networks, it will be well worth the relatively small amount of time you need to invest in learning how to navigate the networks efficiently. Assume that people in the modern world use computers. For example, on the Penn campus we recently encountered a student who actively uses an e-mail account even though she is in a department where typically none of the students have had accounts. When we asked her how she obtained access to e-mail, she replied that she simply took it for granted that any modern university would offer students this resource and asked around administrative offices until she found someone with the authority to issue an account.

Below are listed some of the major sources of external funding for which candidates in the humanities and social sciences may apply directly, using the administrative agency address given. Use this list only as a starting point. Take care to consult the resources listed in the Further Reading section found at the end of this chapter.

7. The Rockefeller and Mellon Foundations

Two major foundations fund numerous postdoctoral opportunities on university campuses. They are the Rockefeller and Mellon Foundations. Students interested in finding out more about postdocs funded by these organizations should write or call for information using the data below.

Address: The Rockefeller Foundation
420 Fifth Avenue
New York, NY 10018-2712
Phone: 212-869-8500

The Mellon Foundation
140 East 62nd Street
New York, NY 10021
Phone: 212-838-8400

8. Individual Advanced Research Opportunities for U.S. Scholars in Central and Eastern Europe[7]

Administrative Agency: International Research and Exchanges Board (IREX).

Address: IREX
1616 H Street NW
Washington, DC 20006
Phone: 202-628-8188

Deadline: Early November.

Award Notification: Late December.

Number of Awards: 55 per competition.

Average Number of Applicants: 200 per competition.

Award Amount: Monthly allowance or one-half salary prorated for grant period; round-trip airfare; family maintenance allowance; passport, visa, and excess baggage allowances; book and photocopy stipend; and housing allowance.

Purpose of Grant/Fellowship and Restrictions: The funding supports research in modern foreign languages and area studies at institutions in Albania, Bulgaria, Czechoslovakia, Hungary, Poland, Romania, and the former Yugoslav republics.

Length of Award: Two to twelve months.

Applicant Eligibility: Applicants should be U.S. citizens or U.S. permanent residents with a command of the host-country language sufficient for research and affiliation with a university as a faculty member or advanced doctoral candidate.

Application Requirements: Applicants must simultaneously apply for Department of Education Grants, such as the Fulbright-Hays, for which

---

7. Based on the Individual Advanced Research Opportunities for U.S. Scholars in Central and Eastern Europe, International Research and Exchanges Board.

they are eligible. This policy assures the most efficient use of existing funds for overseas study and research.

9. Spencer Post-Doctoral Fellowships (Education)[8]

Administrative Agency: National Academy of Education.

Address: Stanford University
School of Education
CERAS-507
Stanford, CA 94305-3084
Phone: 415-725-1003

Deadline: Early January. Application packets will not be sent out after mid-December.

Award Notification: Late April.

Number of Awards: Up to 30 per competition.

Average Number of Applicants: 200 per competition.

Award Amount: $35,000 for one academic year of research or $17,500 for each of two contiguous years of half-time work.

Purpose of Grant/Fellowship and Restrictions: The fellowships are designed to promote scholarship by researchers in education, the humanities, and the social or behavioral sciences in the United States and abroad on matters relevant to improving education in all of its forms.

Length of Award: One academic year or two contiguous years of half-time work.

Applicant Eligibility: Applicants must have received the PhD or EdD or an equivalent degree prior to the deadline.

Application Requirements: A research project relevant to education must be described. Applications will be judged on the applicant's past research record, the promise of early work, and the quality of the project described.

8. Based on the Spencer Post-Doctoral Fellowship Program, National Academy of Education.

10. Smithsonian Postdoctoral Fellowships[9]

Administrative Agency: Smithsonian Institution.

Address: Smithsonian Institution
Office of Fellowships and Grants
955 L'Enfant Plaza, Suite 7000
Washington, DC 20560
Phone: 202-287-3271 or 3321

Deadline: Mid-January.

Award Notification: Mid-April.

Number of Awards: 30–35 per competition.

Average Number of Applicants: 250 per competition.

Award Amount: $21,000 for 12 months; $1,000 per year research allowance; 1 round-trip fare from nearest major airport to Smithsonian facility.

Purpose of Grant/Fellowship and Restrictions: The award is intended to provide opportunities to allow fellows to conduct research in association with members of the Smithsonian professional research staff and to utilize the resources of the Institution.

Length of Award: Six to twelve months.

Applicant Eligibility: Postdoctoral scholars who have held the degree up to 7 years are eligible. The degree or certificate must be completed before the fellowship commences.

Application Requirements: A detailed proposal including a justification for conducting the research in residence at the Smithsonian.

11. Social Science Research Council Postdoctoral Fellowships and Advanced Research Grants[10]

Administrative Agency: Social Science Research Council.

---

9. Based on the Smithsonian Postdoctoral Fellowships, Smithsonian Institution.
10. Based on the Postdoctoral Fellowships and Advanced Research Grants, Social Science Research Council.

Address: Social Science Research Council
605 Third Avenue
New York, NY 10158
Phone: 212-661-0280

Purpose of Grant/Fellowship and Restrictions: The SSRC administers post-doctoral programs in China, the Soviet Union successor states, and Eastern Europe through the SSRC-MacArthur Foundation Fellowships on Peace and Security in a Changing World. In addition, Advanced Research Grants are available to do research in Africa, Japan, Korea, Latin America and the Caribbean, the Near and Middle East, South Asia, and Southeast Asia. Substantial numbers of fellowships or grants are awarded each year. Contact the SSRC for detailed information.

12. Getty Postdoctoral Fellowships in Art History[11]

Administrative Agency: Getty Grant Program.

Address: Getty Grant Program
ATTN: Postdoctoral Fellowships
401 Wilshire Boulevard, Suite 1000
Santa Monica, CA 90401-1455
Phone: 310-393-4244
Deadline: Early November.

Award Notification: March.

Number of Awards: Up to 15 per competition.

Average Number of Applicants: Over 100 per competition.

Award Amount: $28,000.

Purpose of Grant/Fellowship and Restrictions: Support is available for outstanding scholars who are within 6 years of having earned their doctorate (or the equivalent degree in countries outside the United States) and who demonstrate that their work has the potential to make a substantial and original contribution to the history of art.

11. Based on the Postdoctoral Fellowships in Art History, Getty Grant Program.

Length of Award: Twelve months.

Applicant Eligibility: Applicants must hold a completed doctorate (or an equivalent degree from a foreign university). The awards are available to scholars of all nations.

Application Requirements: Completed application form, letters of recommendation, curriculum vitae.

13. Ford Foundation Postdoctoral Fellowships for Minorities[12]

Administrative Agency: The National Research Council

Address: The National Research Council
              2101 Constitution Avenue
              Washington, DC 20418
              Attn: Fellowship Office
              Phone: 202-334-2872

Deadline: Early January.

Award Notification: Early April.

Number of Awards: 25 per competition.

Average Number of Applicants: 100 per competition.

Award Amount: $25,000, plus a $3,000 travel and relocation allowance.

Purpose of Grant/Fellowship and Restrictions: The program identifies individuals of high ability who are members of minority groups that have been traditionally underrepresented in the behavioral and social sciences, humanities, engineering, mathematics, physical sciences, and life sciences and supports their postdoctoral research and scholarship in an environment free from the interference of normal professional duties.

Length of Award: One year.

Applicant Eligibility: Applicants must be citizens of the United States who are members of minority groups underrepresented in formal

12. Based on the Ford Foundation Postdoctoral Fellowships for Minorities, National Research Council.

programs of postdoctoral study and research: Native American Indians, Alaskan Natives (Eskimo or Aleut), Black/African Americans, Mexican Americans/Chicanos, Native Pacific Islanders (Micronesians or Polynesians), and Puerto Ricans. Candidates must be preparing for or already engaged in college or university teaching and hold the PhD or ScD degree. Fellows are selected from major disciplines, including the biological sciences, physical sciences, mathematics, engineering, behavioral and social sciences, and humanities; awards are *not* made in the professions.

14. American Association of University Women American Fellowships[13]

Administrative Agency: American Association of University Women.

Address: AAUW Educational Foundation
P.O. Box 4030
Iowa City, IA 52243-4030
Phone: 319-337-1716

Deadline: Mid-November.

Award Notification: Mid-April.

Number of Awards: 9 per competition.

Average Number of Applicants: 200 per competition.

Award Amount: $20,000 to $25,000.

Purpose of Grant/Fellowship and Restrictions: The organization is interested in improving the lot of women through education. The American Fellowship for postdoctoral work is open to women in all fields and to women of all ages.

Length of Award: One year.

Applicant Eligibility: Applicants must have completed a doctoral degree.

13. Based on the 1994–1995 American Fellowships, American Association of University Women.

Application Requirements: A completed application, including a narrative autobiography, a research proposal, a curriculum vitae, and three letters of recommendation. A commitment to helping girls and women in either or both their academic or personal lives is crucial and should be communicated clearly in the application.

15. National Humanities Center Postdoctoral Fellowships[14]

Administrative Agency: National Humanities Center.

Address: National Humanities Center
P.O. Box 12256
Research Triangle Park, NC 27709-2256
Phone: 919-549-0661

Deadline: Mid-October.

Award Notification: Late February.

Number of Awards: 40 per competition.

Average Number of Applicants: 600 per competition.

Award Amount: Individually determined in accordance with the needs of each fellow. The Center seeks to maintain fellows at their usual academic salary. Travel expenses for fellows and their families are provided.

Purpose of Grant/Fellowship and Restrictions: The National Humanities Center seeks to ensure the continuing strength of the liberal arts in higher education and to affirm the importance of humanities in American life.

Length of Award: One academic year.

Applicant Eligibility: Most fellows are faculty members on leave from colleges and universities. The Center is also open to independent scholars and people from professional life.

Application Requirements: Applicants should clearly state the objectives and significance of the project and the evidence and methodology used.

---

14. Based on the Postdoctoral Fellowships, National Humanities Center.

Further Reading

Annual Register of Grant Support. New Providence, NJ: National Register Publishing Co. Annual.

ARIS Funding Reports. San Francisco: Academic Research Information Service. Frequency of publication varies.

Foundation Grants to Individuals. Ed. Carlotta R. Mills. New York: Foundation Center, 1993.

Peterson's Guides for Graduate and Postdoctoral Study. Princeton, NJ: Peterson's Guides, 1994.

Heiberger, Mary Morris and Julia Miller Vick. *The Academic Job Search Handbook.* Philadelphia: University of Pennsylvania Press, 1992.

Sternberg, David. *How to Complete and Survive a Doctoral Dissertation.* New York: St. Martin's Press, 1981.

Toft, Robert J. *The Grant Advisor.* Linden, VA. Monthly.

Index

This book was set in Baskerville and Eras typefaces. Baskerville was designed by John Baskerville at his private press in Birmingham, England, in the eighteenth century. The first typeface to depart from oldstyle typeface design, Baskerville has more variation between thick and thin strokes. In an effort to insure that the thick and thin strokes of his typeface reproduced well on paper, John Baskerville developed the first wove paper, the surface of which was much smoother than the laid paper of the time. The development of wove paper was partly responsible for the introduction of typefaces classified as modern, which have even more contrast between thick and thick strokes.

Eras was designed in 1969 by Studio Hollenstein in Paris for the Wagner Typefoundry. A contemporary script-like version of a sans-serif typeface, the letters of Eras have a monotone stroke and are slightly inclined.

Printed on acid-free paper.